God Music Family

Written by: Joseph Saddler Jr.

This book is dedicated to me.

A message to those, who know who they are; I love you.

To the others, you only delayed me.

You couldn't stop me.

To my 2 babies, take care of yourselves, each other, and each other's children. Teach your children and their childrens children to do the same. Always.

-Daddy's Watching.

On June 3rd, 2017 Alex Honnold executed one of the worlds most daring fetes by climbing a 3,000 ft cliff located in the Yosemite Valley known as "El Capitan". He did it alone and he did it without a safety net or harness.

I won't be as dramatic as to say his achievement represents a symbol of my life but, I thought to myself; I'll be damned if this isn't a great comparison or metaphor, in the description of my life.

I, from my own experience have come to learn that without great challenges and adversity, one could never really come to learn and know one's self.

As I grew older, began to face my lifes obstacles and mature to my mid-twentys, I used to say; "You have to go through 3 things in life, to know who you really are and what you're made of.

#1. Suffer a great loss

#2. Get your heart broke

#3. Get beatdown physically to where you need medical assistance.

Well, I've been through all 3 and I'm still learning.

On my journey, I supplied myself with 2 means of eternal motivation at a point when I was ready to give up.

My son and my daughter.

They're the fuel that keeps my engine running and I want only the best for them so, I decided to share this story, in hopes I'd be able to offer insight to whomever so chooses to take in this offering.

Here's a bit of advice for all future and present fathers...

The best thing you can leave behind for a child once you've passed on is a good woman. Not money. Don't be afraid to be a father. Don't run away. Fight for your child as you would want your father to fight for you. A childs needs consist of food and your love. Everything else will fall into place.

-Joseph Saddler Jr.

Chapters:

One – **A House on Wheels**
Two – **Forgot about Me**
Three – **Joseph Saddler Jr.**
Four – **Pablo Sosa**
Five – **Hunts Point**
Six – **Grandmaster Flo**
Seven – **The Top Bunk**
Eight – **The S.O.A.L. Survivor**
Nine – **June 9th**
Ten – **Def Jam**
Eleven – **April 12th**
Twelve – **New Respect**
Thirteen – **A Child is Born...**
&
The Dozen Do's

(Flashback indicator: ***)

nowyoucent.com
_____

-Chapter One-
<u>A House on Wheels</u>

On the 13th day of the 4th month in '76 the world was a boiling pot and I was thrown in the mix.

I was ready. My mom, wasn't.

After 9 months of waiting inside her belly, I was ready to make my introduction and caught her off guard. She and my sister Tawanna who at the time was about 2 years old, were home in the Bronx about to eat dinner.

***

A few years prior to my arrival, my mom and dad met in the Bronx New York, on 141st & Cypress Ave. started dating and he moved into her place.

Their second child, my sister Shaniqua, died suddenly exactly one year before I was born. It's the reason my mom, my siblings and I never have, and never will; celebrate, April Fool's Day. The day my older sister died.

The doctors called it (SIDS) sudden infant death syndrome. She was almost 4 months old.

 I never met her, but I will never forget her. My big sister Shaniqua Dawson (S.I.P.).

Three months later I was conceived.

My mom's side of my family is rooted in Savannah Georgia & Alabama, while my dad's roots lie on the Island of Barbados. Bridgetown to be exact.

My father had his first 4 children; Shaniqua, Tawanna, myself, then Satannie (pronounced; Say-Tah-Nee) with my mom. My father ended up making a child with my mother's friend in my mothers home. My mom let her stay in her home because she had nowhere to go. Which is why my half brother S.B and my full blood sister Satannie are just 3 months apart. He then chose to chase his dreams, while my mom was stuck to deal with reality.

***

My mom started to feel contractions & told her friend Darlene to take my older sister Tawanna to my Gramma Ruby's house, hopped in a cab & headed to the hospital. My Aunts; Debra, Barbara, Cynthia and Ulanda came to see me, all 10 pounds of me.

Years later, my mother would give birth to my 2 younger sisters Latoya and Latisha.

When I was about 4 years old, although I was very young, I had a Christmas I'll never, ever forget. Me, my mom, Tawana and my new sisters Satannie and Latoya had stepped out from the shelter where we were forced to stay, to go to the supermarket.

When we got back, we discovered someone had stolen our food, Christmas presents and even stole the tree. I was more confused than hurt. I didn't really understand what had taken place. We were robbed but, I really didn't understand the severity until we woke up Christmas morning without gifts. It was made clear to me then. My sadness instantly kicked in. Even our food was gone.

My mom stayed on her grind, managed to get all her footwork done and we finally had our own place.

I loved to visit with my moms sister, my aunt Cynthia on Andrews Avenue in the Bronx as we did many, many weekends with the usual suspects; Aunt Barbara, her husband; my Uncle O. J., Aunt Debra, (her boyfriend Vincent who years later, was killed in 9/11 Ervin Vincent Gillard S.I.P.) Aunt Patricia, sometimes Samantha and all my damn near 30 cousins.

Aunt Barbara as usual was burning her rolling papers at the dining room table, playing cards with my mom and their sisters, gambling their food stamps or whatever cash they had on hand (Damn, I miss those days).

My cousins and my sisters were outside in the courtyard running around crazy, playing manhunt, tag and the regular hood games hood kids played.

Suddenly, a big bus pulled up, and out stepped… Grandmaster Flash and the Furious Five.

I rarely saw my dad but, when I did, I was the happiest kid in the world. All the kids began to crowd around them. I remember the smell of them like it was yesterday… leather and activator.

I was in the house looking out the first-floor window. I'd just hopped up from my usual spot, my mom's lap, which my uncles always complained about, saying; "You need to let that boy be a man!". I couldn't have been more than 4 years old, lol.

My dad walked in and said hello to my mom. As usual, she looked at him, said nothing, got up and walked into another room. He then picked me up playing with me, swinging me around, took me outside and showed me the tour bus. The Furious took turns passing me around. I hated when it was E-Z Mike's turn because he always slobbered my nose and thought it was so funny, so did my mom and aunt's.

The bus was amazing, it was like a house on wheels.

Visits were never long though. After he talked to my sisters it was time to go.

"So, when are you coming back?". Always my question.

"Soon". Always his answer.

Like always, he hands me this huge wad of cash, leaving me there staring at the back of the bus as it drove off.

It wasn't easy but, aside from everything that went on in my life, I always did well in school.

From 1st to 5th grade, I went to a school right down the block from our second floor, 2 Bedroom apartment at 1768 Weeks Ave. Public school C.E.S. 70.

Weeks Avenue was a wonderland where kids would live through their innocence playing games like manhunt, catch & kiss, skellies, Hot peas & butter, snatch-o-matics; where if you had a food item, snacks, candy or even a juice and you wasn't on point, it would get snatched by one of your friends and you couldn't get mad. To avoid getting your snacks snatched, you had to announce out loud so everybody could hear you before you opened your snack, "Haggy's Down!", then you could snack in peace. The girls would play Hopscotch and double dutch. We'd hydrate ourselves in the summertime with 25 cent juices (quarter waters), get wet at the fire hydrants eat penny candys and go exploring in abandoned buildings doing backflips on dirty mattresses, navigating through all the secret cuts in the neighborhood that would lead us from block to block. The drug dealers in the neighborhood kept us safe, would give us money and buy candy & ice cream for all the kids in the neighborhood. The tough older kids would tell us to go to school if they saw anyone who looked too young to be standing around at certain hours.

We were all poor, had no clue of it and felt like we had everything.

Mr. Mark Singer: an honors teacher, who would years later become the principal of C.E.S. 70 took me under his wing. He taught me how to play chess, made me a tutor in math and chess and stayed my teacher from 3rd to 5th grade.

By Graduation, I was one of the top students and was leaving with honors. My intelligence may have also landed me one of the most beautiful and smartest girls in the school as my prom date.

My mom always said "Respect yourself and others. Especially women". What she didn't tell me was, there are all types of "Women". I think now, she was forcing me to treat women the way she'd wished to be treated.

My prom date Jackie was gorgeous. At this point, I didn't understand; Black, White, or Latino, none of it. I didn't even know Mr. Singer was Jewish, or what Jewish was. All I knew was, I had the most beautiful girl in the world as my prom date. At the time, she was Asian. I'm pretty sure she still is. Jackie and I weren't dating at all. We were just two highly intelligent kids at our prom. We never even kissed; I didn't know about kissing.

We stepped inside and everybody greeted Jackie, as she stepped in with her beautiful dress and her plus one, looking quite dapper if I say so myself.

It was a grand entrance until I suddenly heard screams, just loud screams and shouts of "Oh my God it's him that's Grandmaster Flash!".

My dad walked in right up to me, bent to a squat, excitedly said "What's up son?" and pulled me in for a hug. Thrilled to see him, I hugged him back and said, "Hi Joseph!", as I called him because, I didn't know any better.

My sisters and I also used to call my mom "Paulette", by her first name and, she never corrected us.

***

One day while visiting at our house, my aunt Cynthia, annoyed, said to us "Stop calling her Paulette, call her mommy, that's your mother for Christ's sake". We all looked at Cynthia, looked at my mom, and never called her Paulette again. As full-grown adults we still call her mommy, never "Ma" or "Mom". Except for when my sisters are angry with her, then they call her "Mother", which I've always found hilarious.

***

The kids were surrounding me bombarding me with questions. The teachers just stared at me.

The kids asked things like "Why didn't you tell us?". I was genuinely confused.

"That's enough kids", the teachers ordered, rescuing me from the crowd. My dad got on the turntables, and everybody loved it. I still didn't get what the big deal was. I understood even less because my mom never let us listen to hip-hop music. Her collection was vast but included R&B, Soul, Gospel and Pop, only.

By this time my mother had given birth to the last installment of her 6 children. My sister Latisha, whom we straight up spoiled.

After my graduation, my dad took me to Sylvia's restaurant in Harlem and linked me up with my half-brother S.B.

The following year when I turned 11, he let us stay at his condo in New Jersey for the summer with his new girlfriend; Pam. She'd just birthed my little brother Keith.

Pam was the best. Even though we were at my dad's house, he was never there. Pam didn't really enjoy cooking so; we ate out a lot or microwaved. It was like a party all the time with the same guests; Me, S.B., Keith and Pam. We watched movies, played games and just had an awesome time.

I still called my dad "Joseph" but, S.B. had always called him "Dad". S.B. and my dad were closer as father and son and spent more time together because he was his mothers only child, and his mom was receptive of my dad. As opposed to my mom who was not and had 4 of his children. While there that summer I called my dad "Joseph" like always and he told me to stop calling him that and to call him, "Dad". I slipped up a few more times calling him "Joseph" but, he'd correct me and after a while, calling him "Dad" became a habit. Over the years as I matured it went from "Dad" to "Pops".

That summer, whenever we weren't in New Jersey, S.B. and I would go to my dad's sister in The Bronx, my Aunt Penny's apartment in Betances to chill with her son, my older cousin by about 5 years; Rahmel.

Penny's house was like Yin and Yang because, even though you were guaranteed a full course meal down home style, video games and karate flicks, you'd usually end up being Rahmels unwilling sparring partner. He was in top shape as a child, had bulging muscles and was into all types of bodily harm including boxing, most likely a spirit inherited from my Great-Uncle

Sandy Saddler (S.I.P.), Featherweight Champion of the world through the 1940's and 50's.

Another reason Betances drew me in, was Tanya. I met Tanya and we just clicked. Tanya was my first kiss... and we kissed a lot.

Surprisingly, that's as far as we went and, I never tried to go further, I wasn't even sure what further was. Sex was never a topic.

One weekend, Me and S.B. picked Rahmel up from Betances and he came to spend the weekend with us out in Jersey. We wild out that whole weekend and acted a fool. We hit the gag store on 42nd street and bought a bunch of cool stuff.

We got back to Jersey, greeted Pam and introduced her to Rahmel. He shook her hand, she jumped back and softly yelled, "Oww! What the fuck!". We all started laughing, showing her the "Joid Buzzer". She laughed, started hitting us and promised to get us back. We hung out around the house the rest of the night and did the usual; played video games, chilled and went to sleep.

The next day, Pam snuck out of her bedroom into the living room where we were all sleeping and told us my dad was there. She wanted us to use the joid buzzer on him. We said we would but, we had other plans for him.

My dad is a neat freak. He might even be a borderline germaphobe so, among everything else we got from the gag store, we got a can of fart spray, and a fake pile of shit.
We set it up on the bathroom floor on the side of the toilet and sprayed the fart spray, heavy. Rahmels sinister mind came up with the idea to rub Vaseline on it and the trap was set.

We sat down in the living room, watched cartoons and ate cereal. We heard my dad get up to go use the bathroom, got quiet, and waited.

Seconds later he yelled out… "Whooo took a shit on the floooor?!! Get! In! Here! And clean this shit up nooowww!!!". We were in the livingroom rolling on the floor laughing. I got myself together and left the livingroom wiping the tears from laughing so hard, walked in the bathroom and said, "Okay, relax", bent down, picked the pile of shit up with my bare hand and said, "You happy now?". Me, Pam, S.B. and Rahmel in unison yelled; "Gotcha!!!". He laughed softly and humbly, knowing he'd been got. We all laughed, gave him fives and Rahmel caught him with the joid buzzer.

Days later, S.B. and I'd gotten to 42nd st. to the Port Authority kind of late heading back to Jersey. We were with friends in the Bronx hanging out and lost track of time. When we got to the Port Authority, we were stopped and detained by the Police because we were too young, and the P.A. had a curfew.

We sat in the P.A. Police station for hours scared to death. We called Pam but, she had Keith, and he was too little to travel so late. We called S.B's Aunt Raynette.

She made the drive all the way from the Bronx to Midtown Manhattan, walked in, looked at us handcuffed to the seats and started flipping on the cops telling them to take the handcuffs off. She was not scared AT ALL. She talked to them like she was the cops.

She drove us back to Jersey and I felt it the whole way, that bad feeling in my stomach. Something was way off.

My father said plainly after he gave us one good whack on the ass with S.B's skateboard "Pack your stuff y'all gotta go, you're going home in the morning".

I was devastated.

My father and Pam broke up at the exact same time.

The next day, he dropped us off at the P.A., gave us some money and left. We got on the 2-train headed uptown. Our summer was over.

Throughout the years, I'd barely seen my father but, I'd always hear about him through other people.

He came to pick me up from the neighborhood a few times so people knew who my dad was. He'd DJ'd at my prom so, word spread quickly.

My mom raised me to be good. Only good. What she didn't tell me was there are bad people and things in this world. She kept my sisters and I hid from all of it. We didn't go outside afterschool, and we couldn't have friends over. Kind of like the Italian Mafia, we were around family only, same people, same places, all the time.

We watched The Cosby Show, Family Ties, Different Strokes, Growing Pains, Alf, Perfect Strangers, The Facts of Life, The Jeffersons, Gimme A Break and a bunch of wholesome shows like that, religiously. Television shows with positive messaging about being a good human being. No profanity, nudity or negative messaging AT ALL. There were only about 11 channels to choose from and the television stopped broadcasting at a certain hour during the night and the screen would turn to snow. I remember wishing I was Theo Huxtable. A dad, and a mom? In the same house? Everyday? I thought to myself; Wow, that would be awesome. My mom wasn't super religious, but my homes walls and counters were covered with religious artifacts and quotes which I read and saw each and every day. I was hard wired involuntarily I guess, by my mom, to be a good man from birth.

When I got to Junior High at 12 years old, it was all right there in my face. Fights, sex, drugs and violence. I'd never been in, much less seen a fight. I'd known a lot of the dudes in my new school Diana Sands 147 from my old school C.E.S. 70, and from seeing them around the neighborhood so, we ended up getting cool with each other.

 As much as my mother tried to hide us from it, in the late 80's there was no way she could hide all of this. You name it, and it was at 147 or "The Sev" as it was nicknamed.

Monroe avenue, building 240, was around the corner from Weeks Ave. It's where the dudes I hung with, were from. 240, is a neighborhood not built for the weak, and for the next few years I'd find that out, the hard way.

After a while, I started to hang around the corner from Weeks, on Monroe Ave. at building 240. Only thing was, to hang on 240, I had to be tough. I didn't have a tough bone in my body, or so I thought.

Anytime anybody from 240 saw me, they made me fight. They literally, made me put my hands up, and taught me how to fight. All of them. One by one, for years. Not the older dudes though. They'd entertain themselves by making us fight each other.

I was changing, and I knew it because I felt different. I even started to stand up for myself to my cousin Rahmel. Which only made him go harder but, even he started to give me a little bit more respect.

-Chapter Two-
Forgot about Me

Around 7th grade I lost interest in school. Compared to having fun, school didn't stand a chance.

My mother blamed the environment, including my friends for my new attitude and felt I needed a change. A year later, late 1989, we left Weeks Ave. It hurt me to leave the place I called home for the last 10 years but, by then pain was starting to be a normal occurence.

We ended up staying in John Adams Projects with my Grandmother Ruby.

It was twice as nice because Betances was only a 3minute walk through St. Mary's Park to get to Penny's. She was the designated cook for the holidays but, things soon changed.

Penny had been calling her mom, my Gramma Gina but, she hadn't been answering her phone.

Penny told Me, S.B. and Rahmel to walk over to Gramma's house on 141st & Cypress Ave. and knock on the door. We walked over through St. Mary's Park, knocked like the police, and got no answer. We walked back and told Penny.

She started yelling at us saying, "Why didn't you just call me?! You walked all the way back here just to tell me that?!" and started mumbling to herself about how if she wants something done right, and so on... Rahmel snuck off out the door, so she made S.B. and I walk back over with her.

We got to the bldg., she told us to stay downstairs, and went to get the Super to open the door.

Five to ten minutes later she came running out of the building screaming; "Mommy! Mommy! She's dead!". The Super caught her before she fell to the ground crying. I don't know what happened to my Gramma Gina. She wasn't murder'd and it wasn't natural causes. It was summertime and her apartment was blazing hot. Heat exhaustion maybe? I don't know.

My father showed up soon after. I was sad about my Gramma but, it was also an opportunity to see my dad... I don't remember anything else about it. Gramma Gina (S.I.P.)

We ended up staying with My Grandma Ruby only a couple months because my mom had finally gotten her place.

I was 14 and We were now living at 1151 E. 165th St., in the Hunts Point section of The Bronx just 5 minutes away from the spot, Amadou Diallo would be brutally murdered in a hail of 41 bullets fired at him by the NYPD.

Unbeknownst to me, we were also neighbors with a woman the show "American Gangster" called "Americas Most Evil". Rosalie Garcia was this tiny Hispanic lady everyone called "Shorty". I lived just one apartment above the alleged, Bronx's biggest heroin distributor, and didn't know it. She was so sweet and very unassuming. She always said hi and always had a smile for me. She and her son Manny were eventually sentenced to Life in prison.

I don't know how I passed Diana Sands 147 but, I did. Only thing was, due to my behavior I was banned from the graduation ceremony and allowed to move on to High School.

Wanting to follow in my dad's footsteps, I decided to go to Samuel Gompers High School when I was accepted. I did well in my classes whenever I was there but, I just couldn't stay still.

I still hadn't had sex, but almost had a close call one day the crew decided to cut school and go chill in St. Mary's Park. Tim, Gerald and this dude named La, ran a train on this girl named Dawn in the park.

When it was my turn and they said, "Go head JoeJoe". The first lie that came to my mind was, "I don't feel good". They all busted out laughing, knowing I was lying. They knew I was just scared to do it and I got drilled all the way back to the school.

I'd started writing raps the year before High School when we stayed at my grandmother's house. I'd been to The Apollo once before when my dad and "The Furious" performed at "RAPMANIA". I'd met a lot of the performers like; LL Cool J, Roxanne Shante, Eric b., Biz-Markie and a whole bunch of people.

My 4 cousins also competed at The Apollo. They had a dance crew named, The Dancing Dawsons. I reversed the first 3 letters in their name and came up with "D.D.T." like an explosive, made it an acronym for Doing Damage Together and joined the group. I told them instead of just dancing, let's dance, and rap. None of them knew how to rap. Surprisingly, my cousin Monroe stepped up and said, "Let's do it."

We taught them how to rap, Monroe and I, and wrote all the groups rhymes. At about 11, I rapped privately and sometimes amongst relatives and close friends and started penning my rhymes at 13.

What I loved most about rapping as a little kid was being listened to. I could go on and on. As long as I kept people's attention, they'd listen to me hanging on my every word without a single interruption. At 13, I fell deeply in love with HipHop and began to accumulate stacks of books filled with my rhymes.

I knew nothing about my cousin Monroe rapping, he was super smart and really quiet so, it was a shock to hear and see him spittin. Out of us two, I was playing keep up.

We got Corey aka Everflo, a multi-talented Rapper/Barber/Graffiti Artist, from John Adams Projects in the Bronx to design our costumes. My Aunt Barbara started her entertainment company "Bebra Ent." and managed us. We did a couple shows but, no one showed Barbara or us, any real support. We couldn't keep it together and my cousins gave up. I'd gotten the HipHop bug, I was 13, and I wasn't stopping. I wanted in.

I was happy at Samuel Gompers High School and had my first rap cypher when this dude name YZ, started one in the lunchroom between periods. He had an ill Jamaican type of style, spittin street raps flipping his flows in a way I'd never heard. Then to my surprise, my very own crewmember Major started spittin. If I had to describe his style; I'd say it reminded me of Keith Murray. Right after him my other crewmember Garfield chimes in with his offering. They got me so excited I started spittin right after him. The crowd went crazy, dudes, Puerto Rican girls, Black girls all at the same time yelled "Oh!!!" when I started spittin.

Not at my rhymes though. They were shocked that this little kid had the nerve to even step up and contribute to the Cypher. I was a little, little guy who always looked younger than my age. While all the previous spitters had beards and mustaches, I was under 5 feet, 100 pounds barefaced without a follicle. I'd see the dude "Sonny Cheeba" from the group "Camp-Lo" around the school and knew it was possible to make it because their song "Luchini", was being played on the radio and the song was good.

As I got older, I started to outgrow my mother and the rules she set for me. I was around 16 by now, seeking my independence and abruptly, I would get it. I never disrespected my mother but, I got punished for standing up for Satannie when she stayed out late one night, missing her curfew.

My sister Latoya had been out passed curfew but had made it in before my mom, luckily. Less than 20 minutes later, my mom walked in. She'd been out with her boyfriend Gene. My mom dating was different because she never had men around us. My mom was the "Square" posterchild. She never drank, used drugs or hung out in the streets. I've never even seen my mom smoke a cigarette or drink coffee. I really liked Gene though. He was a great guy and treated my mother very well, which helped her treat us good. He was a single dad raising his young daughter, but pain would creep up and snatch him out of my mother's life. Gene died from something natural. I don't know what, but he couldn't have been older than 40 (Gene)S.I.P.

My mom got undressed, looked in mine and Tawanna's room, both accounted for. She looked in Latoya and Satannie's room. There was Pooky, and there was Latoya, but no Satannie. It was obvious, she was passed upset. We were interrogated but had no real info on Satannie's whereabouts so, she sent me to look for her. I lifted every rock and turned every stone. When I returned Satannieless, my mother looked like she would've settled for whooping my ass she was so angry.

Minutes passed slowly and in walks Satannie. My sisters are all so pretty. She walked in the door with her big earrings and small frame. I knew everything about my sisters. I knew who they liked and who liked them. All their friends and where they went. That's how I was about my sisters. We were all virgins. We had our problems but, outsiders couldn't break our bond. What I said, went. If I told them to walk, they'd run to be on the safe side and I never had to lay a hand on them.

My mother and the whole family sat in my room. When Satannie walked in, my mother stood up. We were all just hoping whatever it was, it was going to be quick. My mother didn't even look at Satannie. She walked straight out of the room, 30 seconds later she came back with a broomstick. I stood in the middle and said, "Mommy wait". She told me to get out of the way but, I didn't move. Satannie stood behind me holding my arm in fear of her imminent ass whooping. I stood firm in between them thinking to myself, from now on things were going to be different.

Little did I know; the difference would be, me no longer being a resident of the household. I said, "No mommy, listen to me". She tried to push me, but I'm older now, still small but, bigger than I was before and I wasn't moving.

It was like I hadn't even said anything or something. Her only focus was getting to Satannie. She said "JoeJoe, this is my child and my responsibility, now move". I said; "You should've been thinking about that before you went out on your little booty call".

In my head, I heard the words "Booty call" in an echo on repeat. I swear, the very second I said it I regretted it and wished it was just my thought or, that she'd temporarily lost her hearing for the moment. Anything! Everybody gasped. Everybody except my mother. She was too busy cocking her arm back. Satannie was no longer the focus. One to the right jaw, one to the abdomen, one to the left jaw, right rib, left rib, face, face, face. Anyone would've felt cheated if they paid money to see this lopsided fight. The only reason she stopped was, she got tired. She walked in the kitchen, picked up the phone, called my father out of breath and said, "If you don't come get him, I'm gonna kill him".

He never came.

She told me to pack my bags and locked me out. I went up the block to my father's cousin; Korduani's house. He smoked crack, but he was cool, plus, I didn't have a choice. I stayed there sleeping on a blanket on the floor. A couple days later I hooked up with S.B., went to Penny's and told them what happened.

S.B. suggested I come stay with him. That would've been the plan but, my dad showed up at Penny's and told us to take a ride with him because he wanted to talk to us.

I hadn't seen my dad in a while and honestly, I started to resent him. I was going through a lot and my patience with him was thin. We said bye to Penny, walked out into the hallway and my dad asked me, "So what's this I hear about you disrespecting your mother?". I looked at him and said, honestly with no disrespect intended, "What do you have to do with it?".

My father backpunched me and I fell down a flight of stairs.

S.B. cried out "What did you do that for?!" and ran down the steps to pick me up. We tried to run but, I was dizzy and fell down another flight of steps. S.B. picked me up and we made it just outside the building, "Come on Joe, run", but I couldn't. My father grabbed me by my collar, threw me in the car and told S.B. to go home, which was right around the corner from Betances, in Morehouse Projects.

On the drive, my father stopped the car by the chicken place near Morehouse about to question me but, I opened the door and got out. He got out, chased me, grabbed me and started punching me again. A few people noticed me and said, "Oh shit that's Joe". My father turned around to the crowd while holding my collar and said, "Yeah, and that's my son!". Everybody backed up like "Oh shit, what's up Flash? Ha ya doin man?". He threw me back in the car.

We stopped again when we got by Southern Blvd. and he said, "Tell me something Joe". I said nothing. He said, "Joe if you don't start talking, I'm gonna raccoon both of your eyes, right now". I don't remember what I said, but I started talking. He took me to my mom and said, "Yeah, he's a little roughed up but he'll be okay". My mother saw I was bleeding, lumped up and started flipping on my father asking him why he did that. I blamed her so, as soon as he left, I went back to Korduani's house.

I started hanging with S.B. on Garrison Ave. everyday inside Hunts Point where he'd moved from Morehouses. I'd only stayed at Korduanis for a few weeks. I came back once to visit him and, somebody told me he was found dead lying face down in the snow. Korduani Bronson (S.I.P.)

My frustration was taking over. I was fighting all the time, never going to class and eventually, got kicked out of Gompers. My mom got me into this school, "Argus Community" for kids with behavioral issues and, I got kicked out of there.

At 16, I got kicked out of my moms, and my aunt Penny's house. My father didn't want me at his sister's house.

One day he walked into Penny's, hunting me down. He walked into the bedroom, lifted me up by my neck, and carried me into the living room while Penny grabbed at him ordering him to put me down.

Instead of putting me down he threw me onto the couch and started hitting me in my face. I began to take hold of his hands and just stared at him angrily while Penny yelled for him to get off of me. He yelled for her to mind her business, I was his son and she needed to "butt out".

He looked down at me in disgust and asked why I couldn't be more like S.B. I said nothing. He added "Damn you aint even half of what your brother is". I shot back "Yeah, and you ain't have nothing to do with it". Angry, he struggled to free his hands from my grip. I felt my face stinging as he stopped struggling and ordered me to let him go but, I didn't.

He snatched away when I loosened my grip, stood up and said, "You aint even worth it".

I said, "You neither". He laughed and said, "Boy you aint shit". I felt myself about to cry but, I didn't, I just ice grilled him. He walked out, Penny locked the door, and then I cried.

Penny told me not to listen to him and told me how good I was. My fathers always hated the relationship Penny and I shared. He was too dumb to realize he was helping to make it stronger because every time he'd knock me down, she'd build me right back up.

I was only at Penny's for a couple weeks because, my father had worked her final nerve and forced her to "butt out". When I went back, she didn't open the door. I sat by the door and eventually fell asleep in the hallway.

I woke up and wandered the streets for a little while, then thought about this place called The Covenant house through a commercial I'd seen on TV, while at Pennys. I didn't last there but a few days because some older dudes that were there convinced me to go into some kid's pockets and take his money. Right afterwards, it felt wrong. The kid was scared, he gave me no resistance but, he just looked so sad. We were both 16. Same age, same size but, this was just wrong on another level. I'd never stolen anything before that, my conscience would never allow me to do it again and I never once, ever, did again.

I got arrested and sent to the Tombs in Manhattan but, the kid never pressed charges and I was released that same day. I was also barred from re-entering The Covenant House.

I tried to go back to my mom's but, it was a wrap.

My father finally came and got me off my mom's stoop. I grabbed my suitcase, and we were off. I thought happiness would be at my father's house on Sheridan Ave. so, I did everything right. I kept the apartment clean, and I even got a job working at Wendy's on Westchester & 3rd Ave.

During my leisure time I'd link up with S.B. and we'd chill at the Saint Mary's Community Center. That's where I met Karen. She was gorgeous. She might have been White or just light skinned with green eyes, full pink lips, ass and hips. She was a 10 visually and I got to have her alone with me at my dad's crib on Sheridan Ave. I still hadn't had sex but, I felt I was ready and, I wanted it to be Karen. I was tired of lying to my family and my friends about not being a virgin but if I didn't, I knew they would make fun of me.

There we were, alone, the two of us and, I still wasn't ready. We kissed, we rubbed and touched but, I was too scared and didn't know what to do. I couldn't ask my friends, or even my father, I'd been lying to him too. I'd never seen a porno or anything and, I couldn't ask Karen, I knew that much. We just sat up, fully clothed in the living room and watched TV.

Hours later my father walked in, looked at Karen, then looked at me. She said, pleasantly, "Hello", extending her hand about to introduce herself.

Saying nothing, my father gently pulled her outstretched hand, up from her seat, walked her to the door opened it wide, cleared the path for her exit, and shut the door behind her. I was stuck.

He came back into the living room and began a soliloquy about how he's Grandmaster Flash, I shouldn't let people in his house, I need to pay attention and to look around.

He packed my suitcase, and we took a silent ride to my mother's house.

When we got there, he got out and I followed. He put my suitcase on the stoop walked back to his car and pulled off. He didn't say goodbye and didn't wait to see if anybody was home. My mom was in her 2nd floor window smirking and said, "See? What'd I tell you?".

I'd been at my dad's less than a week. I abandoned my suitcase, leaving it on the stoop and took the 5minute walk from Longfellow Ave. across the bridge into Hunts Point to S.B's crib. I didn't even care what happened to my suitcase.

I kept my clothes at my moms, but I never slept there. Always at S.B.'s. Everybody decided Job Corp. was the answer. My cousin Rahmel had gone so, my dad got with Penny and signed me up.

Off I went to Oneonta Job Corps. I hated it. It was like everybody just forgot about me.
Other people got letters, visits, packages and phone calls. I didn't like it there but, people liked me.

After 4 Months I was kicked out without my trade certificate because I'd accumulated 82 writeup's for different indiscretions but, I took and passed the GED on my first try before I left.

When I was forced to leave, it was like the whole compound left their classes that were in session to come say goodbye to me before I was put on the bus headed into the village toward the Greyhound. People I hadn't shared two words with were coming up to me giving me hugs and wishing me good luck. This was a good pain. I was touched.

I came back home, still unwanted. A bit tougher emotionally, but still lost.

Since I got my GED I decided to just go to college. I was 17 and, the only thing I'd ever been any good at, was math and rapping. I partially decided to go to college because I didn't have anywhere to live.

I chose accounting because I'm good with numbers and I heard college was the key to success.

My mother & S.B. took me down to The Port Authority.

I gave my mom a kiss and a hug said goodbye to S.B. and got on the Greyhound. I must've been very tired because, as soon as I got on the bus, I fell asleep and had the most vivid dream that I'll never forget.

***

I was in the middle of the desert but, it wasn't hot, and it wasn't sand, just brownish almost orange colored dirt, pebbles and spotted areas of weeds. I just yelled, "Hello!". It echoed back.

Next thing I heard was a loud grumbling, like growling or something. It started to get louder, and it was consistent so, I just started running. The louder it got the faster I ran, then the ground just stopped, and I was falling.

When I looked down, I was high up falling fast, headed toward a sea of brown water, frightened because I can't swim.
Just before I hit, I woke up.

***

I was still on the bus.

I took the dream to mean, me going to college was me moving too fast without really looking, I don't know.

The ride seemed extremely long, from when I woke up. It was taking longer than I expected and the reason for that was, I'd mistakenly purchased a bus ticket headed to Canton, Ohio instead of my true destination Canton, New York.

I got to Ohio and explained the situation to the attendant, she got connected with the college and the school purchased me another ticket. Unfortunately, the bus wasn't leaving until later that night. It was suggested that I go check out the Hall of Fame to kill a few hours before it was time to go.

-Chapter Three-
__Joseph Saddler Jr.__

I looked at the architecture of the building and I was very impressed. The inside was immaculate. I could tell these pieces of history were truly treasured. Nothing looked out of place. I wondered about the celebrity's lives and what they had to do to gain such a prestigious position in history.

I even fantasized I was one of those immortalized beings adored by so many, placed up high on a pedestal for all to see. I ended my pipedream, went, got something to eat, the bus came, and it was time to go.

College, in Canton New York was a blink. I barely went to class, partied; no smoking or drinking except once, where I damn near died drinking Mad Dog 20/20. My friends Norrel and Rodney (S.I.P) from Edenwald in The Bronx had to literally carry me back to the dorm from Potsdam College where I was onstage performing my rhymes, got so happy go lucky I overdrank, when I'd never had a drink in my life.

They took turns carrying me. I was still a little guy. My growth spurt hadn't happened yet.

My roommate a white guy named Lin, cleaned my vomit off the floor and let me sleep it off.

I loved performing my rhymes in front of other colleges, or on their stage, and everybody loved me. I was happy but, it wouldn't last. It was like everybody back home forgot I even existed, just like when I was in Oneonta Job Corp.

I heard a song in college.

The lady sang "Mama may have, and Papa may have, but God bless the child that's got his own".

I was on my own. I had been for a long time. At the end of the semester, I couldn't get a bus ticket home. I asked what family I could, but nobody had it. I was the last student left on the entire campus.

Finally, my mother sent the money through MoneyGram.

It was time to get my own.

When I got home, I immediately linked back up with S.B. and found a job working at Madison Square Garden through an agency called Archer Mgmt Services, making $8 an hour as a foot messenger. I kept my clothes at my mother's house but, I stayed with Raynette and S.B. in Hunts Point. I ran into my neighbor Capone. He was a comedian who owned the barber shop downstairs and had started hosting at Showtime at the Apollo and was even doing some movies with Beanie Seagal of Roc-A-Fella records and Kevin Hart. He was blowing up and inspired me to pursue my shot at making it big.

In Hunts Point it was beautiful because, my mother only lived 5 minutes away walking, right across the bridge and I wouldn't have to go so far away to change my clothes. By now I'd been rapping for 5 years.

I'd never written about sex or smoking weed because I hadn't done either except for the one time I tried weed in Job corp. with Shawn Smith. I hated it.

My rhymes would be hot but, they were more about social issues. I learned about the art of hook making by listening to other artists. I also caught on to the 16bar format. It came natural to me.

My job at Madison Square Garden was a temporary assignment and my time had run out but, I still needed money. I was 18 with expensive habits. Being broke was not an option. I went back downtown to find another job. I was willing to work anywhere at this point.

After my job hunt, I got back to The Point aka Hunts Point and bumped into my man Jim Bob from Homicide Hill, as it was called, on Bryant Ave. I knew J.B. from back in the days when he used to chill in the building next door from my mom's house but, he was from The Point. We talked a little, caught up and he gave me my first taste of the drug game, flipping vials of Crack. I posted up and started clockin.

The money came slow because I was a pitcher doing hand to hand sales.

The money was low, but the risk was high, too high. I made a little bit of paper, gave it to Raynette for some bills since I was basically at this point living under her roof, and quit drug dealing that day. I wanted another job but, being out of work for that short period made me lazy and impatient. I didn't like the low pay and I despised being on a clock having to wake up early but, I still needed money. I was in the back of The Point one day and I saw my friend Jay.

(I'd met Jay aka JayDa-P when I first moved to Hunts Point. We took a liking to each other and became close friends). I told him what was up, he put me on to his man on Lafayette and, we started getting money selling Crack. I was making more money but, it still wasn't enough. I needed more so, we linked up wit this dude right around the corner from my building on Seneca Ave. and the dude started supplying us.

It was more money but, if we got caught, it was also more time because from Crack, we moved on to selling Heroin.

We upgraded and if we didn't want to, we didn't have to do hand to hand anymore. We were managers now getting a 70/30 split so, we could give our workers 10 dollars off each bundle, keep 20 for ourselves and give 70 back to the supplier. I always did my own packs.

I wanted the money but, selling Heroin compared to Crack gave me a different feeling.

It made me feel like I lost my soul. The Dopefiends looked way worse than Crackheads. I couldn't help but feel guilty every time I made a sale. I rationalized by telling myself; it's not my fault, I'm not making them do it and if they don't get it from me, they're going to get it from somebody else, why turn down free money?

I was giving Raynette money and helping with the bills. She didn't know what I was doing but, she wasn't stupid or slow. She tried to talk to me but, anytime I felt too many questions coming I just blew her off. If she asked about the money, I just made something up, she didn't have proof of anything anyway. I was fresh all the time, no job, jewelry, money and had Oj's (cars with drivers) picking me up on the regular. Still, she had no facts but, like I said, she wasn't stupid.

I felt like I was good. I had a nice little amount saved up to where I didn't need a job and felt like I should stop hustling but, in the drug game, it's hard to get out. You may have a lot but, you always want more because there's always more to get.

Raynette told me my dad called, left me a number and said for me to return his phone call. I hadn't heard from him in so long but, I was still excited whenever I got his attention. I called the number back immediately. After some small talk my father got to the point.

The Source Magazine was going to be doing their first annual awards show and he asked if I wanted to go. My response was instant, "Hell yeah!". Anything to get a chance to hang out with my dad. He could've said anywhere, and my answer would've been the same. He said "Good, they're gonna be honoring me with an award but I'm gonna be out of the country and I want you to accept it on my behalf". I said, "Out of the country?".

My balloon of excitement was slightly deflated. It was cool though, still sounded like it would be a fun night. He instructed me to go to my little brothers' mother Pam's house and from there Kev-Dog (S.I.P.) and the driver would pick me up. He said I was to stay close to Kev the whole night. (Kev-Dog was a very close family friend, who also doubled as my dad's security, I'd known him since I was a little kid).

We got to the show and everybody who Kev told I was Flash's son, showed me love. All the faces I'd seen on TV doing that thing I'd come to love called HipHop. They gave me pounds one after the other; Kool G-Rap, Buckshot Shorty, Onyx, M.O.P., Group Home, Fat Joe and many others. I was in the presence of greatness, and they treated me like I was one of them. The show went on after I accepted the award.

I walked through the backstage area carrying the award, headed back to my seat with Pam but, on the way, I got stopped.

He walked up to me like he was waiting to meet me. He looked at me and said, "Daaang, he look just like him, don't he? What's up Lil Flash" and gave me a pound. Kev introduced me and said, "JoeJoe, this is Tupac". I already knew who he was. I told Tupac I'd seen him before and that, that was my cousin Kinte's apartment in Harlem that they shot the movie "Juice" in. He said, "For real man, aww small world". He asked if I was into music too. I said, "I rap too" / "For real? Here man, take my number", and had his homeboy write it down on a piece of paper.

I got back to my seat and told Pam I had Tupac's phone number but, when I reached in my pocket, it was gone. That quick, I'd lost it.

I got outside when the show was over, and people were coming up to me wanting to take pictures or shake my hand. Some people just wanted to talk to me. It felt good, and I loved it but, it was now back to reality.

I got back home to some bad news.

Jay told me that our supplier had gotten arrested, and we needed to chill for a while until things cooled down. We were stressed for a minute but, it wasn't too long before we were back up and running somewhere else.

About a year passed of me hustling & I still hadn't had sex but, you couldn't tell by just looking at me. I'd kissed some girls, I'd rubbed some girls but, I just wasn't ready to take it to that next level.

Honestly, I just didn't care about sex. I cared more about money, and of course, music. I told Jay I was ready to step it up and make my own c.d.

Even though I wanted to make my own c.d., I didn't know how I was going to do it. I needed more information. I went to see my dad and told him what I wanted to do. I wanted to feel like he was in support of me but, the information seemed more discouraging than anything. He was downing the music industry and seemed bitter toward HipHop. He was always rude to his fans. Me on the outside looking in, I would tell him how he should appreciate people taking the time to show him love and wanting his autograph.

As he packed his bag, headed out of town, he told me The Source was having another awards show and if we wanted to, we could come. I said okay, but I remember thinking and feeling like; Forget going to see stars, it was time to show everybody I was one.

Going to HipHop shows to me, had an extra benefit. For me, it was always a chance to be around my dad. This time, S.B. came. He was hyped about getting to meet B.I.G. We'd never met B.I.G. but, we'd seen him a couple of times and went to one of his shows. When "Ready to Die" came out the year before, we both stood in line for hours on 8th street in The Village, waiting to get a copy of the album.

The day of the awards show, we had to go to the V.I.P. entrance in the back of the Garden to get our laminates. We were behind a big crowd and standing right in front of me, I saw a dude wearing denim overalls. I didn't notice right away because his back was turned to me, leaning each of his elbows, on each of the members of Mobb Deep's shoulders. He turned his head to see who was standing behind him, and it was Nas. We were all waiting to go inside and just kept it moving.

One of the security guards stopped me and my brothers by forcefully grabbing my shoulder and pushing S.B. back. He told us the entrance were for staff and artists only. I told him my father was Grandmaster Flash but it did nothing to dissuade him. A guy whom I'd never met a day in my life pushed the security guard back and told him not to touch us again. The guy put the laminates on our necks and walked us through. I didn't know him, but the guy had this huge 3D ring on that said I-God.

***

The next and last time I saw that guy was years later on 161st & Melrose Ave. standing with KRS-ONE, while KRS was conversing with my dad. He remembered me, said not a word and just nodded acknowledgement in my direction.

***

We got inside and saw a lot of entertainers as we went through. We were seated directly behind Faith, Puff and B.I.G., S.B. was hyped. I told him to chill and wait for a good time to talk to B.I.G.

He had a Source Magazine with B.I.G. on the cover and wanted him to sign it so, he got out of his seat and said, "What's up B.I.G. can you sign my mag?".

B.I.G. looked up at S.B., looked down at his feet, scrolled back up, then looked forward like he'd said nothing to him. S.B. stood there for a few seconds, then came back and sat in his seat. I looked at him, he paused a second, stood up, then yelled out, "Yo Rae! Yo Ghost! What's up wit that SharkN***az shit?!". My eyes almost popped out of my head.

B.I.G., Faith and Puff turned around in unison.

The Wu-Tang, who were all seated to our right, started laughing, even the members who didn't rap. I was the one who deciphered to him when we heard "Only Built 4 Cuban Links" that they were talking about B.I.G.

Immediately I hopped up and pulled S.B. out into the hallway to set him straight.

Neither one of us were street dudes but, I'd seen situations spiral out of control over the littlest thing while I was out hustlin. S.B. was a job having, College kid, who was a fan of B.I.G.'s. The things B.I.G. rapped about might've been just rap, but then again, maybe it wasn't. I told him he couldn't do shit like that, and I told him why. He understood. We went back to our seats, and they were all gone.

We watched a few performances and then the big guy with the red shirt went up on stage to accept an award.

I'd never heard of Suge Knight and, this guy wasn't a rapper. He made his speech and caught my attention when he mentioned Tupac's name. When he shot the subliminal that seemed to be directed at Puff, I was really lost but, the crowd wasn't. I thought to myself; this guy is trying to commit suicide.

When Snoop and Dre won an award, everybody started booing. Then I got it. The labels. Bad Boy Vs. Death Row.

When Death Row performed with the jail cells, C.O.'s and a cardboard cutout of Tupac sitting in one of the cells, they fucking killed it. Death Row and the West Coast were coming for the HipHop crown and had the talent to take it. When B.I.G. performed, I cheered extra loud. When he won an Award, I clapped extra hard. It was on, and I was for the home team.

When Puff Congratulated Snoop and Dre publicly on stage for winning their award, it gave me perspective and I started to see. It was the competitiveness of HipHop and wanting to be the best that drove the men. Regardless of where we were from, we were all a part of this great thing. It was ours and there could be many, but only one "best". I was glad I got to see Puff do that.

After the show, the streets belonged to the Wu-Tang Clan.

Rza sat across the street on the sculpture at the Post office with 20 big gold chains on. Method Man came out trying to make his way through the crowd, elbowing overly aggressive fans. The Wu was like 100 deep.

After that, we hopped on the train and headed back to The Bronx.

I started writing a lot more and in between hustling, started coming up with a plan on how I was going to get in. I was 20 and had been engulfed in HipHop in front, and behind the scenes, most of my life. Then it happened.

Tupac was shot.
Days later, he was pronounced dead.
Tupac (S.I.P.)

I'd already felt his and B.IG.'s beef had gone too far.

Radio and magazines were adding fuel and finally it'd reached the point of no return and a person's life was lost.

Six months later B.I.G. would suffer the same fate.

I remember the day clearly; S.B. and I were asleep. It was early in the morning and the sun was beginning to rise. Raynette frantically came into our room, waking us from our red bunkbed set yelling, "JoeJoe! S.B.!, wake up! They killed Biggie!". Not fully awake, we both hopped out of our beds running, stumbling to the living room in silence to hear the news on the radio.

We sat on the couch listening, not saying a word through the audio confirmation. It wasn't a dream. The rapper Ice-T was expressing his disgust stating, whoever did that was "some suckers", a West Coast artist. Snoop expressed his displeasure, another West Coast artist. I was confused. Weren't we supposed to hate each other? My confusion broke instantly.

We'd all lost someone. No matter where we were from, we were a family. The HipHop family had lost another member, and the family was pissed.

People close to me actually cried, talked about B.I.G. and how great he was. He was a representation of us, and he was gone. The loss of these two very significant people in this thing of ours was a dark period that changed mine and a lot of peoples lives, forever. There it was... unavoidable pain, even in the hiphop game. B.I.G (S.I.P.)

My 21st birthday was coming up and I was hyped. S.B's girl Addis came over with her best friend Leonella to see him. Her friend had the biggest titties I'd ever stood close to. We started talking, getting to know each other and hit it off. She came over a few more times, and we started to get closer.

This time S.B. took Addis with him to the store. Once we were alone, we got to kissing, rubbing and she told me to wait. She took that beige turtleneck sweater off and unleashed the titans. They were perfect. She took her bra off, and her nipples sat up on two huge mounds. I was ready. I sucked them, squeezed them, cupped her ass, licked her neck, undid her zipper and there she was... Naked. I, still not totally confident in myself, turned off the light, got undressed and put the condom on just like I'd been practicing. I layed her down, felt her slit and slid inside saying goodbye to my virginity. I pumped about three times before I came.

She pushed me off her and said, "Wait, wait".

I took off the condom and turned on the light expecting the worst. Expecting to get my feelings hurt. I was ready. Ready to experience some new kind of pain. When I turned on the light, she was curled up on the bed holding her stomach, saying in a higher pitch than her normal, "Damn, you did it too hard, shit! Was that your dick? I felt that shit in my stomach, just wait a minute". She didn't even know I came. With that boost of confidence, when she was ready, I put another condom on, and we got it back poppin... Slowly.

Right after our supplier got knocked, Jay got us in with his man from 163rd & Kelly St. a block away from where the BIG PUN (S.I.P.) mural would later rest, just outside of Hunts Point and we'd been going strong ever since.

After my 21st birthday, my father sat down with me because he'd found out somehow that I was hustlin. He felt like I needed to do something else. His concern was a welcomed change but, I resented him, and I was still living with a lot of pain.

My father and I barely knew each other. Besides concerts and confrontations, we spent zero time together. I knew nothing about his personal life; his favorite food, what foods he didn't like, his first love, first time having sex, nothing. I was just glad whenever I got to be around him. His attention, negative or positive made me feel relevant. He suggested the Army. I put up a little resistance but eventually, I gave in.

I don't know why, but after all these years, he also wanted me to have his last name. Since birth I was Joseph Dawson. I'd wanted his last name since I was a little kid and asked plenty of times, once I found out the significance of having your father's last name but, he never budged so I stopped asking. I agreed with his request. So, for my 21st birthday I became Joseph Saddler Jr., lost my virginity, and figured out how to get out of going to the Army.

I'd spoke to somebody during casual conversation, and they told me their cousin was supposed to be going to the army but had gotten denied for having marijuana in his system. I kept quiet about my impending enlistment and thought to myself "Bingo". I'd tried weed for the first time with Shawn Smith when I was in Job Corp. I hated it. It wasn't my thing but, it kept me out of the Army. My father was pissed.

A couple weeks later, Jay and I woke up early to hit the block. We had it mapped out. The night before, we'd gotten everything ready and had been checking the temperature of the block, just walking around chillin. The plan was set.

-Chapter Four-
Pablo Sosa

We clocked in the next day and sold damn near $3000 worth, in about 2 hours.

I'd seen the detectives drive by in the dark blue Impala and one of them look directly at me so, I walked around the corner and circled the block on foot. I got back down the block and, as soon as I saw the coast was clear, I started serving. Not even 2 minutes passed before I felt a hard ass push from the back. I hit the ground, looked over, saw some blue New Balances, looked up and saw it was the same stout, white-faced detective who looked right in my face.

They put the handcuffs on me, sat me on the ground, went into my stash and found the last 7 slabs (10 slabs or glassines $10 a pc. in a $100 bundle).

I was almost done.

I looked across the street and they were coming out of the building with Jay in handcuffs. They crossed the street and sat him down, right next to me.

When we got to the precinct, I didn't know what to expect and I was scared. The detectives pulled me out of my cell, brought me in the back, showed me pictures of people I knew and asked me questions I knew all the answers to. They told me they wanted to help me but, they needed my help. I'd never been in a situation like this, and I just wanted to go home. As I looked at the pictures, I saw the faces of people who did, "help me".

If it wasn't for them, I wouldn't have had anything I'd possessed. For me to repay them by putting them in the situation I was in, just so I could get out... felt wrong. Dead wrong. Nobody made me do what I was doing out on that corner.

I looked at the pictures and said, "I don't know them". Once he was convinced that I was of no use to him the detective kneeled close to my ear and whispered aggressively "Well I hope you like prison, because that's where you're going.", roughly lifted me up and put me back in the cell.

They let Jay go because I said I didn't know him, gave him a ticket and charged him with trespassing. They let me go the next day because it was my first offense.

(R.O.R.) is what they called it, Released on your Own Recognizance. I was thrilled. Glad it was all over. That was easy.

Me and Jay went right back to the block. It was nothing else we could do. We had no money.

A couple months later I was chilling on 163rd and Kelly talking to my homegirl Kia who lived on the block I hustled on. I was sitting on S.B's Mountain bike and out of nowhere, detectives sped up to the corner, hopped out of their car and yelled "freeze!". Instinctively... I melted.

I ran through a schoolyard and the cops cut me off by driving against traffic up a one-way street.

Even though I hadn't been hustling all that day, I just threw the bike down and ran.

I got to this building and the door was locked.

This door was never locked.

I pressed the bell but, as soon as I buzzed, the cop put the gun on my head, right behind my ear and screamed for me to get down on my knees. I complied. He cuffed me, walked me to his cruiser and put me in the backseat.

When he and his partner got in the passenger and driver's seat and closed the door, I said to them "Yall'd better not do nothing to me because my aunt knows exactly how I looked when I left the house this morning". The cop in the passenger seat turned right around and punched me dead in the middle of my face.

The 41st precinct had grown a reputation for being corrupt. Back in the 60's and 70's, they were known as "Fort Apache" and the stories of their tactics spread throughout the Bronx, I was screwed.

This time, there was no coming home. I'd missed my court date from the first time I was arrested and got remanded; A hold in the system that makes you ineligible to have a bail or bond. The same dudes, the cops tried to get me to turn on came to bail me out but, it wasn't happening.

My Co-defendant was somebody I'd never met a day in my life named "Pablo Sosa".

***

(I'm laughing my head off at this moment because, at the time, I just didn't put together how bad of a fake name that was. I'd never heard of Pablo Escobar and hadn't seen the movie Scarface yet).

***

The police report said "Beck St." I'd never hustled on, knew anybody or even been on Beck St., and anyway, they arrested me on 163rd St.

Turns out, the police were chasing some skinny black kid on a bike. I was sitting on a bike and that kid got away. They put me in his place.

They shipped me from The Bronx House holding facility, to Riker's Island. I see why they say "Nobody's Smilin on Riker's Island". I was there about 7 months before I got sentenced and had only 2 physical altercations from the date I got arrested. The first was at The Bronx House where this kid tried to walk my sneakers out of my cell while I was sleeping, but I caught him. I acted like I was still sleeping and as he walked out of my cell, I grabbed him from the back and banged his head on the toilet. The second incident was on Riker's.

I was sent to C-73, 2-lower main. This incident was a shock to me because, me and the dude had grown a relationship and were cool. It was over something small but on the island, if you let the smallest thing slide you became food.

The kid threw a plastic chair at me. I caught it mid-air before it could hit me, but still. When I approached him to see what his problem was, he snuffed me (an off guard, punch to the face).

At that exact moment, the C.O.'s came in to do the pedigree. That's' the count on Riker's, to make sure every inmate is accounted for.

We kept it low, but I was heated.

This dude from University Ave. in the Bronx named Barkim was like, "Fuck that! Wait 'til after the count and fuck him up!". That was my plan. That, or he was going to have to fuck me up. Either way a confrontation was imminent.

We all crammed into the day room and walked out one by one as the C.O. (Correctional Officer) counted us. I saw the kid and his man in the corner laughing, when it was my turn to walk out. I went, sat on my bed and waited. Waiting for the last man to leave that day room. When Barkim came out, he sat on my bed. I never let anybody sit on my bed or lean on my locker but, my focus was elsewhere, plus Barkim was pledging allegiance.

The last man walked out, the C.O. left, and I headed straight toward the dude. Barkim grabbed me and said, "Chill, take it in the bathroom". I was about 120 pounds, the kid was just a little bit bigger, but in that moment, I was totally illogical.

We went in the bathroom and about 10 seconds later, the fight was over. One punch. He was laid out.

I tried to go buffet on him but, his man wasn't having it and grabbed me in a chokehold from the back, but quickly released me, raised his hands as if he was being arrested and said, "You got it. That's my man I was just breaking it up". The crowd drew the C.O.'s attention. He picked his man up and we all walked out the bathroom like nothing had happened.

I saw Big Chuck in the mess hall sitting with about 30 Bloods gang members. The fight had just happened, he was housed in a totally different unit, but he already knew about the fight. Don't ask me how.

He stood up, called my name and said, "N***az is actin up?!". His whole table looked and waited for my response. My table did the same, including the dude I'd fought with.

Chuck was about 5'8", and 200lbs. of solid muscle, his fingernails may have even had muscle. He was the first person I'd ever seen do handstand pushups in the center of the dorm like he was leaning on a wall. He Breakdanced downtown with my cousin and that's how I'd met him. We shared a house when I first got to the Island. Shortly after reacquainting with him, I was transferred to a new house. I looked at my house, looked at Chuck and said, "Nah, everything's cool". Everybody reassuredly went back to eating. Other than that, I was a rapper, and that's what I was known for.

One day I got a visit. I didn't know what was up because so far, no one had come to visit me, and that's how I wanted it. No expectations. I'd gotten letters and a couple of packages from Raynette, but this visit was weird. The visit process wasn't going as I'd heard visits went. They walked me to this little cubicle and left me there for about 5 to 10 minutes.

Next thing I saw was one of the most beautiful faces I'd ever seen. It was my little brother Keith's mother; Pam. Pam had become a Parole Officer so; she got the hookup and came to see me.

Since we'd lived together in Jersey when I was younger, we'd never lost touch. Me and S.B. would spend weekends at her apartment in Manhattan playing video games with Keith, listening to music, watching movies and stuff.

When I saw her, I just hopped up "Maaa!!!". With my arms outstretched trying to hug her. She pushed me and said "Boy, calm down. You trying to blow it up? Sit down!". I was just so excited to see her face.

We sat down at a table, facing each other and she just looked at me with her lips in a pout shaking her head from left to right in disappointment.

She had no idea I was selling drugs. I just put my head down. She said "Pick your head up, you're here now and this is what it is. Are you okay?". I slow nodded, yes. She asked me, "What happened?". I told her the truth. We talked for about an hour and a half.

She told me she left me some money and picked up all my jewelry from property. She also told me I could call her every weekend, collect, and I did, all the way up until I went home. She had to leave and just that quick, our visit was done.

I gave Pam a kiss and a hug, she left, and I went back upstairs to jail.

Jay and S.B. came to visit me a few weeks later.

We were cracking jokes, catching up, and they left me some money, clothes and underwear. It was a short visit. My imprisonment was killing my vibe. I just wasn't used to it yet. I wanted to leave with Jay and S.B., but I couldn't. I gave them both pounds (a handshake) and went back upstairs, after my strip search.

I woke up one morning and was called for court. Everyone who had court had to step into the hallway. I started seeing people I knew from the street. We weren't allowed to speak and had to walk single file against the wall to this room where we waited to be handcuffed and put on the bus. These dudes that the C.O.'s referred to, as "Predicate Slasher's", were loaded on to the bus first.

They had to wear these things on their hands that looked like boxing gloves. Their wrists and feet were shackled, and they were led on to the bus alone one at a time.

They were placed in a separate compartment on the front of the bus surrounded by a cage while the rest of us sat side by side, one wrist cuffed to another inmate. I was handcuffed to a white kid and apparently the 2 guys behind me were "Latin Kings".

One of the Predicate dudes was a "Blood", and he was nuts. The way he talked to those Latin Kings sounded like he had a genuine hate for them, but I could tell they'd never met.

The Latin Kings returned the verbal assault and mixed it in with gang signs from their free hands. Them not knowing each other made no difference. If either of them had the chance, they'd make sure they made the other feel the worst kind of pain. The Blood's rage was enflamed by the King's signs, it's like the Blood was speaking another language, like he was possessed, it was almost demonic. He couldn't throw any signs with those boxing glove looking restraints and he was chained top to bottom.

The C.O. warned them that he would kick them off the bus if they didn't quiet down. Everybody hated the last bus because, it's more wait time and more time sitting handcuffed.

I couldn't believe what I'd just witnessed.

We got to the Bronx Supreme Court Building from Queens, were placed in the cells with about 20 people, got uncuffed and waited to see the Judge.

While we were waiting, the Blood that was on the bus, was placed in a separate cell by himself, still cuffed. After a few minutes, the Blood just yelled out, "Peace Almightyyy!" and at least 30 voices from unseen faces yelled back "Peace Blood!". Then they went on to do this whole call and respond chant.

I love music, but this was deeper, darker and deadlier. I felt it in my bones and what they were saying gave me chills. It went on for a few minutes and ended with them repeating, saying "Bdaaat! Bdaat!" Then it was quiet. The C.O.'s didn't even bother telling them to be quiet so I'm guessing this must've happened before. Then it started.

The language.

They had their own form of communicating, yelling back and forth indecipherable code known only to the members of the Bloods.

After about an hour of waiting, one by one, names were being called.

They finally got to my name, and I was escorted to another section of the building to different cells, for another dose of waiting. This cell was in an area where when your name was called you got to speak to your lawyer before going to see the Judge.

I had a "Public Pretender" aka a Public Defender named Mr. Raymond. A public defender is a lawyer appointed to you by the very same court that's trying to prosecute, convict and send you to jail. I learned about all that years later but, the feeling I got when I first met the man was; I just did not trust him.

I was new to the system and, although I lacked the knowledge on how it all worked, I felt he wasn't on my side. Everything he said and his demeanor showed me he did not have my best interest at heart. He wanted this over and done as quickly as possible. He didn't even ask me what happened, or if I was innocent. I couldn't believe he was trying to get me to willingly go to jail instead of getting me to fight.

I got offered something called a plea deal. A plea deal is offered by the court to avoid a costly trial, but you've got to be willing to go to prison. To me, it was dirty and very underhanded.

I got arrested for the first time and I had no drugs on me. They found it close to where I was standing and I did do it so, I guess I could deal with that. The second time I was arrested, I was completely innocent.

It was time to face the Judge. They brought me through this little door and led me into this huge courtroom.

The Supreme Court. Funny, this didn't seem like a "Supreme" case.

Even the courts had their own language, just like the Bloods. It was all about me, and I didn't understand a word they were saying.

$1\frac{1}{2}$ to $4\frac{1}{2}$ years for both charges. I was already in jail for 7 months and that time counted in the sentence of the $1\frac{1}{2}$, so I'd be out in less than a year unless I got hit at the parole board for negative behavior during my incarceration.

The Judge asked me things like, "Am I pleading guilty of my own free will?" and yadda, yadda. A bunch of shit I don't remember. I had to say out loud, I was guilty, for the court records. Even for the crime I did NOT commit, and there it was. I was sentenced and I knew exactly how much time I was facing.

It was a long bus ride back to Rikers. I finally arrived and was placed in the Y-me pen because the standard cells were full, then the pens where we waited to be strip searched. Someone called my name "Yo JoeJoe!". I looked across the way, and in a different cell, I saw my homeboy, Kareem.

Kareem is the only young dude I knew personally that owned a Bentley. I knew him from Morehouse Projects. I said "Oh shit! What the fuck is you doin in here?". He threw his hands up in an, I don't know gesture and said, "I don't know. What you doin in here?". We both just busted out laughing. He hadn't been there long, and I could tell he was fresh off the street. His red hat and red barrettes at the end of long boxed braids, red Coogi sweater and red sneakers told me what it was.

I looked around his cell and all the dudes were dressed similar, 1997 was a strange year. I'd never heard of the Bloods, but here, it was no avoiding them. We talked over all the loud chatter until it was time for me to go. I told him I'd see him on the block, and I was off.

I hated getting strip searched and wondered to myself; what kind of man takes a job where one of the duties is looking up another man's ass, then got the nerve to tell that man to turn around, lift his nuts and cough, smh.

The mystery was over. So was my stay at Rikers Island. I had to admit, it at least felt good knowing how much time I was facing on that long bus ride, headed to the next Correctional Facility in Ulster County.

I got there and compared to Rikers Island it was very clean. The food was better, and it was a little bit more space in the bedding areas. I wouldn't be there long though; this was just one of the many stops I'd make before reaching the final facility.

My next stop was "Elmira State Prison". That tall ass wall let me know, you're not in jail, this is prison.

Thankfully, I didn't have to stay.

Right after court on Rikers, I got a call from my P.D. Mr. Raymond and he offered me a program called "Shock", where instead of doing hard time and facing a parole board, having a chance to be denied, you could complete this program and be home in 6 months. I said, "I'll take it!".

He said, "There's a lot that comes with this program, you're going to have to…", I repeated, "I'll take it", home in 6 months, was all I heard.

Elmira state Prison for me, was only a stop to exchange the shackles and handcuffs and to pick up new inmates, who looked more than happy to be leaving that place. They were also eligible for the Shock program. As long as you weren't convicted of a violent crime and you were sentenced to less than 3 years on te front of your sentence, you could be eligible for the Shock program.

Next stop; "Lakeview Correctional Facility".

Lakeview was a part of the Shock program, but it was where every inmate eligible for the program had to stop first before being sent to the actual compound that they would be spending the next 6 months. At Lakeview they basically got you prepared. They shaved your head bald if you had hair, and made you stand still while they threw this powder on you that was used to get rid of any kind of crazy insects that might be hitchhiking.

They gave you your pamphlet that stated all the do's and don't's and explained what was expected of you. I knew jail or prison was not for me and I was never coming back. It reeked of pine, funk, men, and no girls? "Awl hell nawl!", I wanted out. We finally got up to, Summit Shock Correctional Facility.

After the Introduction I finally got it. I may not have understood right away but, I felt I had an idea of what the Shock program was about. It was partially designed to test your restraint. You were pushed to your limit mentally as well as physically, waking up at 5 in the morning every morning for Physical Therapy or, "P.T.", rain, sun or snow, to see how you would respond.

Everyone was tested, and many broke down. Some couldn't control their anger, fought the Drill Instructors or, "D.I.'s", or other inmates and were sent to prison to do their full time.

Depending on the severity of the incident, you could get a new charge and have additional time on top of your sentence. It wasn't easy for me. Making the transition was a process and I went through a lot; physically, mentally and emotionally but, I hung in there.

By this time in my life, pain was like one of my arteries, just another part of me but, so was my talent for writing.

Each dorm was broken down into "Platoons", from "A-bay", all the way up to "E-bay". We were E-bay with about 30 inmates to a dorm.

Our D.I. Mr. Schrader gave us a couple days to come up with a 30second sound-off that represented "The War Dogs" as we were called. Each Platoon had one. Ours was the best. I knew that because the Superintendent of the whole facility, a Puerto Rican man from the Bronx named Mr. Nieves told us so.

I wrote everything for our platoon; our sound-off, cadences that we would sing on our morning jogs and everything we brought out to the blacktop where we did our P.T.

As inmates, we were all required to work. We'd pick a job and had the option of picking a duty on the compound we felt was the most suited to us. I chose to work in the administration building filing paperwork.

-Chapter Five-

Hunts Point

One day while working in the "Admin.", one of the staff members tried to blame me for an important document mistakenly being put through a paper-shredder.

I didn't do it.

In Shock, you're only allowed to refer to yourself as, "This inmate". You had to request permission to speak, have no eye contact with anything you said, and your sentences had to begin and end with "Sir" or "Ma'am", unless you were talking to another inmate.

I said to Superintendent Nieves "Sir permission to speak sir". Nieves replied, "Speak inmate".

"Sir, this inmate did not put the paper through the shredder sir".

He said "So she's lying? Are you calling my staff a liar?". I said, "Sir no sir".

He said "Okay, so you did do it?".

I said nothing.

He said, "You're Sanders? Right?", calling me by the last name I was arrested under. He continued, "Do you know what it means if I know who you are?", again, I said nothing. I'd already felt where this was heading.

He got close to my face and said, "It means you've been nothing but trouble. Go pack your bags, you're finished!".

He was right. I was always in some shit doing one of those stupid ass punishments, standing outside for hours holding a dinner plate, doing the "Rock Pile", or carrying a log, just always something. So as loud as I could I said, "Sir yes sir!!!", turned around and went straight to the dorm. At this point, I just didn't give a fuck what happened.

The first 2 months of the program, you're a green hat. The next 2 months you're a red hat. The last 2 months, a gold hat. I was a red hat with my 22nd birthday coming up in less than 1 week.

I went and packed my bag preparing to go to jail... ahem, excuse me, Prison.

As I was packing, Mr. Schrader walked into the dorm. Usually, you had to stand up and stand at attention when a D.I. walked in but, I just sat on my fully packed bag. Mr. Schrader: a White man who looked to be about 50 or 60 years old, stood about 6'6", pipe thin with a blonde mustache that covered his top lip and, always wore long straightleg sweatpants that covered his belly button.

For whom ever is reading this, just so you know, Mr. Schrader can do more sit-ups than you, and will out-jog you, day or night. Period.

He asked me what was wrong, and I told him. He turned around and walked up to the administration building leaving me sitting alone on my bag. When Mr. Schrader returned, he walked into the dorm room with a swift stride and yelled, "On your feet inmate!". I stood up and he said, "Grab your bag, let's go".

This was it for me. All that time wasted. I wasn't going home early. I was going to prison, a sentence inside of the sentence I was already serving.

We left the dorm, walked out onto the blacktop and standing there was Superintendent Nieves.

The newly arrived platoon was also walking up getting ready to do the 6 Mile jog all new platoons do when they first start. I stopped, looked at them and tried to pick which ones I thought wouldn't make it, just by looking at them. Mr. Schrader said

"Sanders, I spoke to Mr. Nieves and he's willing to give you one last chance". I said "Okay! Thank you, thank you".

I could've said it a thousand more times if I had to. Shit, I was in my 4th month. Mr. Schrader cut me off and asked me, "Sanders, I'm gonna ask you this one time, and I want to know the truth… Did you shred the paper?".

I looked at him and I wanted to lie. I just wanted to get it over with, but I couldn't do it. Minus the "Sirs", I looked him in his eyes and said, "No Mr. Schrader, I did not do it". He said "Okay", patted me on my shoulder ushering me toward the dorm and said, "Put your P.T. gear on, you're doing the 6 Mile jog again".

Now, when I did the 6 Mile jog the first time, I was glad when it was done and promised to never run again… In life. My legs were like noodles when we finished and didn't stop hurting for days after.

Today however, it was different, I'd never worked out before Shock. By that day, I'd been working out and running 1 mile every morning for the past 4 months so, I was ready and said, "Okay". I went for my bag to take it back in the dorm to get changed up, but Mr. Schrader stopped me and said, "Take your P.T. gear out of the bag here. You'll take it inside later, IF, you finish the run".

I took my gear out, went to the dorm, got suited up and came back to the blacktop ready to go.

Mr. Nieves had been standing there the whole time and never said a word, until now. "Get the bag Sanders". I questioned; "The bag?".

He said, "Yeah, you're gonna run with the bag, and if it touches the ground, you're gone". My bag had to weigh at least 50 pounds. It had everything in it; State boots, toiletries, all my coats, clothes, paperwork, underwear everything but, I wanted to go home. The platoon started to jog. I picked the bag up, threw it on my neck, took a step, then slammed it to the ground.

I said nothing and started pacing as tears started to well up.

It was heavy, and the strain of having to do what I was told, instead of what I wanted to do plus everything else at stake, was all additional weight.

I stopped pacing and stood there staring down at the bag.

Mr. Schrader started his shit, "Pick that bag up Sanders and stop being a little pussy!". He just circled around me, as I stared down at the bag. He continued "You're gonna let that fucking bag beat you?!, Voice of the War Dogs?!... What do you wanna do? You wanna go to prison, or do you want to go home? Come on, gimme a mile Sanders! Pick it up!". Then I did.

Mr. Schrader started jogging along side me, and I didn't think about the weight on my neck. I thought about all the times I'd ever felt defeated. All the times I'd ever felt pain. I wanted to win.

Halfway back I'd almost dropped the bag but, one of the kids from the new platoon ran over and caught it. I got about 5 minutes of rest, while about 5 members of that platoon switching off, taking turns with the bag got a taste of that weight. That was until Mr. Schrader said, "Sanders, we don't need no punk ass platoon carrying a War Dog's weight now do we?". I shouted; "Sir no sir!!!", kept stride, grabbed the bag and threw it back up on my neck. I felt so weak. Only thing I was running on was Mr. Schrader's voice.

The platoon had made the turn ahead of me, heading back to the blacktop. Every staff member and every inmate stood out there waiting for the platoons arrival like always whenever a new platoon finished the 6 Mile jog.

I heard the claps and the cheers for them as they completed their run.

As Mr. Schrader and I came around the corner and they saw me running with that bag on my neck they went crazy. They clapped, they whistled, stomped, cheered, banged on the walls and yelled "Go Sanders go!!! You can do it man!!!". I saw Mr. Nieves standing right where I had to stop, and stop I did, right at his feet, dropping the bag and lying flat on my back.

He said calmly, "On your feet inmate, and stand at attention". I popped up and stood firm, no eye contact, hands at my side, heart beating, clothes dripping with sweat and my body hurting. Mr. Nieves said, "Sanders, I respect you, but don't think you did something big here. What you did was for you. If you really want to prove something to yourself...", ordered me to look at him, got close to my face and said, "...do something for somebody else". I took it in. Forever.

He continued, "You earned your spot, so you can stay. Go wash up and hit the mess hall". I did.

Inmates usually get 3 minutes to shower and 3 minutes to eat. That day, I got a total of 15 minutes to do both. I got to shower alone as opposed to being surrounded with 30 buttnaked wet males, and I ate in an empty mess hall by myself.

I thought about the run, the cheers and everything that took place as I sat there and ate, and it occurred to me.

See, everybody knew me because I was a knucklehead but, after that day, everybody treated me different. They had to, because I felt different, nothing was the same, including my behavior.

Before Shock, when I was home, all I did was wake up, walk out of my door, did shit during the day, went home, went to sleep, rinsed and repeated.

After Shock, I learned that I mattered and the choices I made, made a difference in not only my life, but the lives of people I'd never meet. I'm important. I count.

Two months later, it was time to go home. On the day that I was leaving I woke up kind of down because nobody had sent me clothes.

The facility gave me "State issued" clothing; the gray Corcraft sweater, those hard ass cardboard denim jeans and state boots. On the bright side, at least I was going home, but first came the ceremony. I know it was jail but, I felt as proud as I would've, had it been my graduation because I'd made it through when so many others hadn't.

All the inmate's families were waiting, as we marched in sync eyes forward to the blacktop. First person I saw was Pam. I'd been calling her collect every weekend just like she'd said I could. Next person I saw was S.B, and then my father. I said my part in the cadence and they all started cheering. I was so glad to see them because I wasn't sure if anyone was coming.

I wanted to ride back to NYC with my dad, but he didn't offer, so I didn't ask. We just had no connection. I rode with Pam.

We went to Pam's house to talk, catch up and chill. As usual my father was busy and couldn't join us.

I was now 22 and I always had a crush on Pam's sister Nina since I was a kid but, she's family so I never crossed. I was too young anyway but, she was always so gorgeous to me. Pam's sisters were both beautiful, as well as her mom. Nina resembled the actress "Halle Berry", but that's my little brother Keith's aunt so I never acted on it.

An hour after our arrival, Nina came over. She came in, gave me a hug, told me how good I looked, and I returned the compliment. We all sat and talked about what we wanted to do with our lives.

Pam and Nina wanted to start a clothing company. Everybody already knew what I wanted to do.

Pam and Nina had a prototype of a shirt they'd designed and asked me to model it for them. I had on a T-shirt, but Nina said it would look better if I wore it without the tee because it was as they called it, "High Fashion". It was a nice silk, pink, long sleeve button up shirt that fit nicely on me. They told me to walk back and forth and keep the shirt unbuttoned.

I reluctantly took my first stroll across Pam's room. Everybody admired my form, especially S.B. because I'd always been super-skinny. He said "Damn sun! What was they feedin you?". Working out for all those months made my body more defined and I ate everyday, so I put on weight. I went in about 120 pounds and came out 162.

I've never felt comfortable with my body since I was a kid because I was so welted and skinny. Even though I'd gained weight I still felt the same. The attention kind of embarrassed me so I just put my shirt back on and changed the subject.

Keith was somewhere with his buddy Christian playing Basketball so, I didn't get to see him that day. I would be leaving Pam's soon because I had a curfew. As a Parole Officer Pam wasn't cutting me any slack and kept watch of the clock. She hopped up and said, "Oh yeah", walked into her room and came back with a small black velvet bag containing my chain, ring and my bracelet. We had to go but before we got on the train, we stopped by Ms. Howell's, Pam's mom. She wanted to see me.

The first thing she said when she saw me was, "Boyyy, you got big, you're so handsome", gave me a hug and a kiss on my cheek, rubbed the sides of my arms and said, "You look good". I loved Pam's mom. I said, "You too, you just get more beautiful every time I see you". It's true.

Back in Hunts Point.

I got home and saw Raynette for the first time. She was always fresh dressed head to toe, gorgeous and full of fire. I was so happy to see her and even happier to be home. We rode around all day and she took me to her old stomping grounds on 145th street in Harlem or "45th" as it was called, where she chilled with her "Bout it Bout it Girls!". We stopped by a store on the strip so she could meet up with her homegirl Kim. Kim's brother D-Ferg owned a clothing store over there. He designed his own clothing named after himself called Ferg. It's the first time I'd ever heard the term "Black Owned". He was so cool and gave me and S.B. some free shirts that day. Sadly, shortly after that he'd passed away. I don't know what happened to him but, it wasn't gun violence or anything like that. Just glad I got the pleasure to be inspired by a young black entrepreneur before he left us. D-Ferg (S.I.P).

S.B's cousin Yoshi came over for a visit. What I didn't know was, he'd been staying there off and on while I was locked up. He was from Harlem. It was always cool to spend time with him and his 3 brothers on 130th & Convent in Harlem.

***

Harlem, or "Mecca", as some people called it, was a place where the Black man could walk amongst his own people with pride.

We were surrounded with the culture that was the blood, flesh and bone of the people. Harlem has style that's very often imitated, and attempts are frequently made to duplicate it. When the culture couldn't be copied, or captured, it was studied, and subsequently stolen.

I grew up seeing that Black people were creative in nature. "From the root to the fruit", we were forced to be. Even in my own life-experience of my own creativity, I hear and see people doing and saying things that didn't make it off my cutting room floor. We come up with the "Fly" on a fumble. I used to be amazed by my capabilities until I learned where I came from and realized... I'm a Black man... it's in my blood. I hadn't been rapping seriously as far as taking the steps to take it to the highest level but about 2 years, but I was nice, and everybody told me.

Everybody on 130th & Convent, or "The Hill" as they called it, showed me love. Including popular D.J. S&S who lived in the neighborhood.

I was given passage to walk around by myself because Yosh bragged to everyone that Grandmaster Flash's sons were his cousins. Without that, we were just outsiders on a block filled from corner to corner with straight goons.

Even though we had the free hood pass, we were not exempt from the endless snap sessions that would occur out of nowhere.

There were regular wardrobe and bang-bang (bootleg) inspections and a bunch of other shit that came with chilling in Harlem with Harlem dudes.

There was no room for the "Broke". I was about 16 at that time and stayed fresh as a habit so it was one less thing for me to worry about. Still, fresh as I was, one day Me, Kinte, S.B, Bill(S.I.P.), Yosh, Z and E walked to 2-5th aka 125th street, so we could get some Popeye's chicken and I was the last in line to order.

I ordered a 2 pc. and fries. The lady pointed with the tongs at the pieces of chicken, so I could pick which one I wanted. She picked one up and I said, "No, no not that one, I want the big one". Bill then shouts, "Oh he said he wants the big one!", and everybody busts out laughing repeating, "He wants the big one!".

I'm like "What the fuck is wrong witchall?". They kept laughing, saying "Nothing", out of breath from laughing so hard. I didn't get it. The lady handed me my bag, I checked it and told her she forgot to give me my sauce. Again, "Oh, oh, oooh" and a crowd of laughter. This time, I was pissed and genuinely annoyed because, I wasn't in on the joke but, I knew it was one happening, and I was the mark.

We got back to the hill to the basketball courts. This was the basketball court G-Money shot his shot in New Jack City. Whenever I saw the movie, I'd get excited because I knew the park and played in it many times throughout my childhood. Harlem was full of stars, hood and otherwise. Aaron Hall was a friend of my family on my little brother Keith's side. He knew Pam and her sisters and had even bought my brother Keith a puppy once. He also knew Yosh, even though Pam and Yosh had never met.

One day Aaron came to Harlem for a visit, saw Yosh and his homeboys, the brothers; Z and E chilling in front of the building, walked up and showed them love.

When Aaron found out I was related to Pam, he showed me love too. I'd heard a lot of his music, but to meet him was an experience. Nothing at all like I would've expected. He was straight hood.

We ended up riding around with him from that afternoon 'til about 5 in the morning. I don't know how it came up but, we were all chilling on 2-5th by Saint Nicholas Projects and Aaron challenged me to a foot race. He had a kennel built into his truck so, he put his dog up, took his shoes off and got on his mark.

Barefoot on the concrete, at 1 in the morning, I raced Aaron Hall for an entire block giving it my all and he smoked me. He jumped off the curb and everything. Maybe I should've took my shoes off too.

 Later that night, we went to a club which I amateurishly fell asleep in, up in the balcony (never been a club dude. Still not.). He left with two gorgeous ass women, left us to drive his truck and headed straight into the projects like he wasn't the celebrity that he is. He looked at me and said "Hey Flashjr., better luck next time", then dipped off.

Two other movies were shot on the Hill. Wesley Snipes movie, "Sugar Hill", and "Juice". This guy named "Crazy Sam" was in front of the building when they were filming Juice and told me that he had a part for me, all I had to do was go to the roof and jump so he'd know I was dedicated. He was joking of course. He was a friend of my dad and I'd met him back in the days when he worked on "Video Music Box" with "Ralph McDaniels".

Every time I see Juice I trip. They filmed 80% of that movie on the Hill and the end scene was shot right in Kinte's house. More and more I began to love the entertainment business, and wanted in. I'd never heard Tupac's music before Juice but, I'd heard he was a rapper and started to take notice.

I finished up my Popeyes and noticed quietly, that while everyone was talking, they repeatedly said the phrase "No Homo" or "Pause" midsentence, and I didn't know why.

I didn't want to seem like too much of an outsider so, I asked a kid who I'd heard saying it and asked him what it was about thinking my ignorance would be kept a secret but, Chopan was a Harlem kid. Fresh top to bottom, couldn't have been older than 11 or 12 but had the swagger of a dude twice his age.

We were at the "Bitties" with the other imaginary Dunk Kings. The Bitties were basketball hoops about 7 feet high, that had the shortest guys doing the tallest tricks.

After he got in a few snaps (insulting jokes) he broke down what the "Pause/ No homo" thing was all about. I didn't know whether to laugh or be pissed off all over again. One thing I knew for sure, I'd be watching what I said, and probably wouldn't be speaking as much.

Chopan was an intelligent kid and had a bright future ahead of him. I often wonder what he'd be like today had he not gotten shot all those years before. From what I understand, Chopan, someone a churchgoing woman would call, "a baby", was hit by a stray bullet.

When I came over that weekend to the news, it caused me a great sadness. Chopan to be so young was ahead of his time and gone way too soon. Chopan (S.I.P.) little brother. I gave my condolences to his brother Tuscon and told him to pass it on to his family.

I've always hated guns. The first gun I saw in real life was a revolver hanging out of Clarence from 240's, sweatpants pocket.

The first gun I ever touched was my father's 357 Magnum when I stayed with him in New Jersey.

I knew of their power and destruction and never touched one unless I was afraid with no other choice. I'd heard Lenny shot himself and wondered, what he could've been going through to make him do such a thing. I knew Lenny since a kid, we weren't friends but, he's from Hunts Point so we shared some of the same friends. Guns have a ripple effect when fired. I knew that. I know that. Lenny (S.I.P.)

***

HipHop, and music in general has always been a big part of my life. I could say it's genetic through my mother and father but, that may be a stretch. HipHop was different now from when it first started. Yosh left, I did my pushups I was accustomed to now because of Shock and went to sleep.

I woke up the next day to report to my Parole Officer, got the rules, gave urine and bounced 'til the next week.

One of the rules was to get a job.

Getting a job was one of the stipulations of my parole or I would get violated and sent back inside. I got in this program called CEO for parolees newly released. A van would be by the Sears

Fordham Tower on Fordham Road in the Bronx to pick us up. We would do things like; pick up trash on highways with a poke stick, pull weeds from the grass, other types of manual labor and get a $30 check at the end of the day. After a couple days of that, I started to get stressed.

What I was thinking, and my solution, had a high-risk factor. I went to the back of Hunts Point and it looked different. It wasn't as active as it was before I got locked up and I got the update on what it was.

Everybody told me that the cops came through and majority of my friends got swept up by the police in an operation called "The Bloody Point". It was on TV news, they showed me the newspaper article and as I read it, it was re-affirmed to me how real this selling drug shit was. These were people I'd grew up with. It was too close to home. I kept up with my parole and continued going to CEO for about a month. All I did all day was stay home and write raps after work. That was my plan. Be a big rap star and get rich while I was at it. I felt I was better than everybody I knew about, signed or unsigned.

In 1998 it was rare to meet a person that rapped and even more rare to meet someone who was actually good at rapping. Compared to now whereas you can throw a rock and hit someone who calls themselves a rapper.

Hip-Hop to me for the women turned into Hoe-Hop. For the men it was Hate-Hop. Hate directed at ourselves. Hip-Hop to me was created to bring our people together. A large percentage of what I was hearing now was degradation and division. Things that were once underground and out of reach of children were placed in the mainstream readily available for all to consume; pornography, prostitution etc.. The Underworld took over the surface.

-Chapter Six-

Grandmaster Flo

My dad invited me to a DJ show going down the same night, hosted by Maria Davis. She had this show she'd throw at clubs called "Mad Wednesday's". I'd heard of her, but this was my first time meeting her.

We got there and the show was crazy. The DJ's really did their thing. One of the DJ's Roc Raida (S.I.P.), told me how he's my brother because everybody said he looked like my dad. He killed the turntables and was one of the best sets of the night. People showed my pops a lot of love and respect. As usual the effects trickled down to me. I even gotto leave with some free c.d.'s and "Mitchell & Ness" jerseys.

I woke up the next day in a funk because I was still obligated to obtain employment, had no leads, and those $30 CEO checks just were'nt cutting it.

I went down to the Wall Street area and found a job doing the same thing I did at The Garden, as a foot messenger for Deutsche Bank across the street from The World Trade Center buildings.

I hadn't seen anybody on my mom's side since I'd been home, until I was walking down Southern Blvd. and bumped into my sister Satannie. I was so excited to see her.

We sat in the Pizza shop for hours talking and catching up. She was staying in a woman's shelter in Brooklyn and was about to have her own apartment through this new program called Section 8.

She told me how much she missed me and asked me if I could come stay with her. It seemed like fate. She told me I would have my own room as opposed to the one I shared with S.B. in the 2-bedroom apartment in Hunts Point, with Raynette occupying the other. Satannie said I'd be responsible for paying all my own bills. She was 8 months pregnant with my nephew and looked like she was ready to pop. She told me who her baby's father was and even though I didn't know him that well, I remembered him, and he always seemed like a good dude.

Before she left, she invited me to her Baby Shower and told me if I wasn't there, she'd be sending out a search party to come and find me.

I told her I would most certainly be there. We gave each other a kiss and a hug, which was totally different. My mother never hugged, kissed, or told us that she loved us. I guess it just wasn't her thing to say it. I think Satannie and I were just caught up in the moment, overjoyed about seeing each other. I know I was.

Satannie and I growing up, were always the closest out of all my siblings, which may be why we argued so much. I was the older brother trying to tell her what to do, while she was the younger sister trying to rebel.

It was time for the Baby Shower.

When I got there, my aunt Cynthia was already there standing outside. She was really shocked when she first saw me because she watched me grow, I'd always been really thin, and she hadn't seen me in years. She saw me from the back, sitting on her son Shawns bicycle that I'd borrowed from him just a few minutes before. She couldn't believe it was me and gave me a 60 second hug. My sister Latoya pulled up, then I saw my sister Tisha, my sister Tawanna, my aunt Penny and 100 other guests. Everybody was there.

I looked to my left and saw, my mom. I hadn't seen her in years. I was cheesing so hard my face started hurting, so was she.

She started tearing up saying, "Damn boy, I didn't even know you was my son, you got so big!". I gave her a long tight hug and a kiss on the cheek. I kept my arm around her shoulders for about 20 minutes while she went around introducing me to everyone I didn't know, proudly introducing me as her son. I made my way to the corner by the music. There he was, in position at the turntables, my father. My cousin Shawn made his way up to the tables, I said what's up to my dad and grabbed the mic.

Shawn and I went back and forth spittin verses until it ended up being just me. My father kept switching up the beats and I killed each one of 'em. My father always knew I was nice. Now he knew I was serious. Someway somehow, I was getting "A Deal".

After I finished rhyming, I blended back in with the party. I spotted Satannie, who looked like if you bumped her, she'd give birth. I gave her a hug, talked to her fetus and after a few hours, the night was over.

I woke up the next day and took a shower, letting the water run on my head thinking about the day before, still trying to figure everything out. I heard a knock on the bathroom door. Raynette yelled, "JoeJoe! The phone. It's your father!".

The first thing he said to me after I said "Hello?" was, "So you're ready?". I said, "Ready? Ready for what?", he hung up.

It reminded me of a time in Morehouse Projects when I was a teenager and Raynette's friend Sheba came up to me while I was sitting on the benches and said, "So JoeJoe, you ready?". Me not having the slightest clue of what she was talking about I said, "Ready for what?". She just busted out laughing and walked away.

Since I wasn't for the mind games, I called him back and asked him if he would just be straight up and say exactly what was on his mind. He said he wanted to talk to me.

"They call me JayFlo the rap pro, smash any competitor cut you out like an editor chop you up and etcetera!"

Rapping was what I've always wanted to do. It's what I've always done. No matter where I was, or who I was with, I did it.

At 22 I knew it was going to be my career and I had the perfect person to get me in the door.

No matter who I was a fan of, they had somebody that got them in the door; B.I.G. had Mr. Cee, Jay-Z had Jaz-O, Ja-Rule and DMX had Irv Gotti, Snoop Doggy Dogg had Warren G, RUN-DMC had Russel Simmons, Jermaine Dupri had his dad. Shit, even Beyonce had her dad, and the list goes on.

No matter how talented someone was, it wasn't enough to get in the door. My dad gave me the baton and a cassette tape full of beats to write to.

I'd helped my father build his in-home studio and he had every piece of equipment necessary to create an album of sonic perfection. I started writing right away.

I didn't like the beats. They weren't that bad but, they weren't that good.

I'd finished recording about 8 songs before I came up with the title; "Grandmaster Flo" since it was all his beats and all my rhymes, I mixed JayFlo with Grandmaster Flash.

Recording the album was relatively easy, especially with my pops coaching and teaching me about inflections, how to emphasize on certain parts and speak clearly, all the technical things that come with recording. I'd never recorded for an album, and it was nothing like recording for a mixtape, but I was a natural. I followed his instruction and took right to it.

We bumped heads during recording because of a song I was set to record called, "Where I'm from".

I let the beat come in and it started with a Bass on the hook. I let it ride a little, and then I came in; "Ballaz Cop Drop's and uh/ Thug n****az drop cops and uh/ Ballaz cop drops and the thugs drop cops and the Ballaz cop drops/ Where I'm from! / Them thug n***az drop cops/ Where I'm from them...".

My pops stopped the engineer and cut the music shouting, "Woah! Woooah! Noooo! Joe!!! You're talking about dropping Cops?!!! Unh unh, come out the booth Joe, you gotta write something else".

I left the booth and tried to explain to him that, that's not what I was doing but, initially he wouldn't listen.

After a few minutes, I explained to him that I was telling a story about something that an older person told me concerning the corruption in the 41st precinct, reflecting on life just like I do with anything I write about. I was told that; policeman's bodies were found in the back of Hunts Point floating in the river. Is it true? Who knows? It made for a dope song, so I wrote it. Not once in the song did I say anything negative towards law enforcement. His curiosity allowed him to let me record the song.

He still didn't like it. He told me all my music had too much of a dark feel to it, and that I needed to come up with "A stupid song". He played something by an artist he felt like I needed to emulate. He spoke of how Down South music was fun and playful and I needed to lighten up. I told him I wasn't going to rap like that and began naming Southern artists that didn't rap like that and told him them dudes he played was straight up garbage. He gave me an ultimatum and I ended up recording the worst song I'd ever wrote in my entire life called "Over Here, Over There".

If I never hear that song again, I'd have had a great existence. That was the last song we'd record, and the album was never finished.

Recording the album had been easy because I had a lot to say but, there were just certain things I wasn't willing to do.

When I finally left Raynettes house, it was hard.

I was closing an important chapter in my life, I wanted Raynette to know I appreciated and loved her. I didn't have the courage to tell her to her face so, I just wrote her a letter, thanked her, grabbed my things and headed to my new home with Satannie on 183rd and Morris.

I moved in to Satannie's 3-bedroom apartment with nothing but clothes.

I loved being there with my new nephew Bishme so I spoiled him and loved doing it. I continued to see my father and we talked about completing the album. He said he needed to talk to me and for me to come out to his house in Central Islip, Long Island. I took the L.I.R.R., as I'd done many times before, but this visit was different. He played the albums songs we'd completed and as he played them, handed me a recording contract.

What my father didn't know about me was, I despised contracts of any kind, still do. I feel it relieves you of your freedom to make choices and puts you under someone else's control. A leash. I was totally offended. I'd heard the rumors about my father, "The Furious 5" and "Sugar Hill Records". I asked him "Why would we need a contract?"/ "It's just business Joe, it's how you do business". I told him I'd need somebody to look at it and he gave me a look of disgust.

He expressed how he'd already spent money recording the album, and how he'd gotten Satannie to let me into her home, so how could I not trust him. I never knew he and Satannie even spoke about that, and his behavior made me feel like I was doing the right thing.

I stood firm and he calmed down, still trying to get me to sign. He told me he was being Honored again at "The Source Awards". This time it was going to be in Los Angeles, and he wanted me to come with him. I didn't want to go. To tell the truth I was tired of HipHop shows, and everything they came with. I hadn't seen my father much throughout my life except for at concerts, backstage and in the audience. I'd leave the poor people in the ghetto I've always lived in, to visit the rich and powerful. Coming from the bottom where you're given nothing, to be around the famous who had more than enough but were still given things for free was starting to take its toll on me. I reluctantly agreed.

I was still working across the street from The World Trade Center as a foot messenger and everything was going good at Satannie's house. I started to notice something.

All Satannie's, and her babyfather Bishme's friends smoked weed. I didn't. the house was always clouded with weed smoke, so I got an idea. I hadn't sold drugs or did any criminal behavior since I'd been home but, I'd heard you couldn't get any jailtime for selling weed. I bought a half a pound and started selling only to family and friends. I was stacking cash fast, so I hooked my room up and hit Satannie off with some extra money on top of helping with the bills. I was so cash set, from time to time I'd even give some of my weed away.

One day my cousin Rahmel came through to check me. I hadn't seen him in years. I'd heard he was hustling O.T. (Out of Town) and was making money, but I didn't know what he was hustling.

He'd made a new baby out there and everything so, I figured he must be doing well. We chopped it up (talked) for a minute and he offered me to come with him O.T.

I told him I would pass because he told me he was selling Crack. After going to jail I knew I'd never do anything that could send me back.

He told me I could make $800 off an 8-ball of rock cocaine. I knew I could get an 8-ball for $80. I looked at him with a what kind of an idiot do you take me for? face. I knew he was lying, or he was about to say, "Nah I'm just fuckin with you". He said "Joe, it's yours if you wanna come get it, I'm not playing with you". I looked at him, thought it over, went, got the 8-ball and we hopped on The Metro-North.

Long story short, he wasn't lying. In less than 1 hour I had it flipped. I gave him a pound, hopped back on the Metro-North, and never went back.

There's no way you're making that much money, that fast, and the cops aren't somewhere watching, is what I told myself. Not too far down the line Rahmel got bagged (arrested) and sentenced to 4 years. He was never the type to lie down though. He'd fought and won multiple cases representing himself in court. This time, I guess they must've had him cold.

Jam Master Jay (S.I.P.) presented my father with his award. I stood way off to the side on the Source Awards stage waiting for my father to introduce me to the world.

Not only did he not introduce me, but he also said nothing about "The Furious 5" and gave no S.I.P. respect to Keith Cowboy.

***

Keith Cowboy is an original member of the Furious Five and the first rapper to diss other rappers (by name) publicly, on a Major release. Keith went at LL Cool J, Whodini, and even RUN-DMC at the height of Def Jams run. The song is called "Yo Baby" off the "On the Strength" album Same album the Furious 5 rapper Raheim was SINGING on a song called "Flygirl", for any rapper that thinks they created that. Keith was onstage at the Infamous Queens crew The Supreme Teams party, sharing the stage with Melle Mel. He was my fathers best friend. My little brother Keith carries his name. Keith Cowboy (S.I.P.)

***

I thought to myself, what's wrong with this dude? Why isn't he taking any action?

Before we went up onstage, I contemplated giving my demotape to Will Smith or Russel Simmons. I had it in my pocket, and I was sitting right next to them. I decided against it due to my blind loyalty.

We exited stage right and were herded through a few interview stations.

KRS-ONE's station was one of them. He had a L.A. radio station and wanted me to spit for him, so I got ready. My father stepped in took his attention away and herded me away from the station.

Me and S.B. were dressed similar and the celebrities all were in multiple snapshot frenzies with other celebrities to capture the moment in time. Everybody wanted to hop in a pic with us; Treach, C-N-N, Jazzy Joyce, Outkast, they all knew who my father was.

Andre 3000 bent down to my ear before whoever snapped the pic and said, "Whatever you do, make sure it's what YOU, want to do".

I don't know why he chose to say that to me because, he could've just as easily passed that jewel to S.B. who was standing right there. Whatever the reason, I never forgot it, and still apply it. I'd bumped into Scarface and Yukmouth from The Luniz earlier in the day at a store that doubled as a liquor spot. I asked if I could take a pic and Face said, "Hell yeah come on N***a!" We got to the show, Face spotted me in the building and pointed to me when we caught eye contact. I pointed back.

The 1999 Source Awards to me was ran by the Los Angeles Crips. They were all over the place.

They had a huge bus of their own and a big dude who had the word "Crip" tattoo'd on his bald head, which at this time was taboo. Even the cops looked afraid.

HipHop stars were getting pressed, and I saw a dude get robbed at the urinal right next to me. The dude gave no resistance as the robber casually lifted his chain off his neck by the charm, while the victim just kept peeing.

We got back to the hotel and while my dad was at the desk checking us in, Eminem and D-12 walked up. We exchanged greetings and I told Eminem how dope I thought he was.

We went around all introducing ourselves and his homeboy Proof (S.I.P.) invited us to a surprise birthday party they were throwing for Dr. Dre at the Playboy Mansion. My Pops shut it down quick when we told him, "No Joe, I need you right here".

We got upstairs and I flipped, "What's goin on?! Why aren't you telling anybody about me?! Why didn't you say who I was on the stage?! Why aren't you talking about the album?!". He calmly said, "Joe, you don't know what I'm doing, let me handle the business".

I fell back for a few reasons. Number 1, he was right, I don't "know the business". Number 2, this is my father. Number 3, I trusted him.

All I saw was missed opportunity after missed opportunity. I talked about it with Kev-Dog and Angelique; my little sister Christina's mother who was also with us on the trip. I got to do no networking and made no connections.

I got home totally unsatisfied. I didn't know what to think and I was beyond confused.

I got back to Hunts Point where I still hung out, even though I'd moved to Satannie's. Everybody saw me on TV and asked me a million questions.

After I told them what happened, they were equally unsatisfied, "You should've just snatched the mic". One person said, "Why you aint just start spittin?". "Why this?" and "Why that?".

-Chapter Seven-
The Top Bunk

About a week after the awards show, my father calls and asks me if I signed the contract, and it hit me. Now it all made sense.

I said, "No, this contract is not okay, and my lawyer couldn't believe it was my father who gave it to me"/ "Joe, it's a standard contract".

HipHop is so educational, that if you listen well enough, you don't need to go to school or even college to become successful, well, at least it used to be.

The singer BabyFace wrote hits worth millions, Master P owned his label, Diddy owned Bad Boy, Rick Rubin and Russel Simmons, The Eazy-E and Dr. Dre beef, Roc-A-Fella records, Jermaine Dupri, even my dad claims he got ripped off. I did the knowledge surgically and paid my dues by the age of 23.

I told my dad; I wanted a percentage of the label. I had a fleet of talent and a pack of hungry wolves I could bring into the fold. My father laughed as if I'd just told a joke but, I knew my worth, even if he didn't. He hung up and it was the last I'd heard about it from him.

Simultaneously I was abruptly kicked out on the street by Satannie.

She'd been telling me, Big bishme and my father that she wasn't getting money from any of us, while collecting money from all of us. I confronted Big Bishme, and he said he was about to confront me but stayed out of it because im Satannie's brother. He admitted he'd just given Satannie $300 for an abortion and later found out she was lying about being pregnant. My father confronted me about not chipping in and I showed proof she was getting money from me. I even showed him where she ran up a $900 phone bill talkin to Dionne Warwick and her psychic friends. Satannie was getting free childcare, Con Edison, WIC, Food Stamps no job and had Section 8. She felt I'd brought an end to her money triangle, punched me in the middle of my face and threw everything I owned out into the hallway.

I stayed at my cousin and his girls crib sleeping on the couch but, I wasn't recording anymore so I had extra time on my hands.

I started chillin more with Jay, mostly indoors with some girls or something because as convicted drug felons we'd be arrested simply for being in each others presence in public. It was cool hanging out but, I just didn't want a bunch of girls. I wanted, One. I still had music on my mind though. I tried to figure out what my next move would be.

I headed down the block to my aunt Cynthia's on Burnside and saw my cousin Ricky. There it was again, the same as every other neighborhood I'd chilled in since I'd got home. Only this time it was one of my very own relatives.

My cousin Ricky was head to toe draped in "Blood" attire, and just a few feet from him was Gary, and the man who allegedly started it all, O.G. Mack.

I said what's up to Ricky and my homeboy Bockey, also a member of the Bloods. I on the other hand was dressed like their rivals, the "Crips" rocking royal blue from head to toe. I felt and saw all 20 plus Bloods looking at me but once they were all given my non-gang affiliation and neutral status by my cousin Rick and Bockey, I was taken off the menu.

Creston Ave. was 1 block over from where I lived so, it was nothing to see "Set Reppers" or hear about "Who did what" or "Guess what happened?".

Creston Ave. was ground zero for the east coast Blood movement but, I knew how to mind my business and never stayed in one spot too long so, I never got caught up. I talked with Ricky and headed upstairs to see my aunt Cynthia.

One day after hustlin, I was chilling with my cousin and his girl and met her best friend, Rita. She resembled Nia Long when she played in Love Jones. We kicked it and just ended up in the livingroom talking.

I went over to visit her at her place a few times but always had somebody with me or, she had her friends already there. I'd never gotten a chance to be alone with her. It was getting boring pretending like we didn't want each other so I just grabbed her hand and pulled her toward her back bedroom. Rita stopped me at the door and said, "Unh unh, what are you doing?"/ "Nothing"/ "I'm not going in the room with you"/ "Why?"/ "Because I'm not"/ "Listen, I just wanted some privacy, I promise, I will not try anything."/ "Lies"/ "Wow, for real?"/. She put her hand firmly on my chest, looked me in my eyes and said "No. Stop.". I stared into her pretty brown eyes, pulled her hand slowly off my chest, down to my hard dick, never losing eye contact. She gripped through my sweats, went from base to tip, and said, "Okay let's go".

We went in the backroom, closed the door and I started stripping her like she was a meal, and I hadn't eaten in days. She stopped me and said, "What are you doing? We can't get naked in here. What if somebody calls us?". She paused, told me to be quiet, opened the door, checked to see if anybody was listening then said, "Come here", and pulled me into her closet. I pulled her pants down around her thighs, turned her around and slid in from the back. No condom.

The first time I'd ever had unprotected sex.

It felt so good I started to long stroke. She pushed me back, in between her moans saying, "Not so deep". I'd tell her I couldn't help it, in between mine. She said, "Oh my God, I'm gonna scream, then in succession whispered, "No, no, no, no", pushed me and pulled away saying, "We gotta stop". We just stared at each other, leaning on either side of the closets wall, breathing hard with our pants down around our waist. It couldn't have been more than 5 minutes, and I didn't cum. She said in a soft tone, "Come on, pull your clothes up, oh my God everybody's gonna know", and starts fixing both our clothes simultaneously. She walked out the closet and said, "Don't come right out, just wait here for a few minutes and then come out. I'm gonna go in the bathroom". I just looked at her, same "Devilish smirk" and started toward her. She put her hand on my chest and said "No, we can finish later". I tried again and this time she shortened her response, same firm hand on my chest, "Later", opened the door, looked around, and snuck out.

After a few minutes, she came out the bathroom and I was already in the livingroom. Her friend was like, "Unh unh, whatchall was doin?". I smiled and said, "Nothing".

When Rita came out of the bathroom, I went in to go freshen up. We all hung out, ordered pizza and wings and watched The New York Knicks.

Hours later, I went in the front room, and everybody was knocked out drunk and high. Rita was out on the recliner. I woke Rita up, grabbed her by the hand and guided her by her waist into the backroom.

I stood behind her, kissing her on her neck, rubbing every secret place through her clothes.

While she rubbed my head, my hard dick poked her backside through our clothing, and I unbuttoned her jeans. I licked her cheek, and my tongue found its way to her mouth. She turned around to face me keeping our lips locked. I rubbed up and down her back as she rested her arms around my shoulders. I squatted to her 5feet and came back up to my 6feet with a hand full of ass cheeks. She took my shirt off and I began undressing her, we stopped kissing only when we had to. Finally, there we were, Naked like the juice.

She was in top form. Perfect breasts that weren't too big, not too small with dark pointing nipples and I took a mouthful of each. I laid her down, kissed her lips, found her already moist dripping slice and slid in slowly. It was the best I'd had thus far. We went on and on, non-stop. In, out, kissing, licking, panting and sweating. I wanted to switch positions, but we were constricted by the space the bottom bunk allowed so, we got up and went to the top bunk. It was like we never stopped. We'd been fucking for at least 2 hours before we fell asleep in our own puddle too exhausted to clean up. We woke up all throughout the night to go at it again and again.

The weekend was approaching. I woke up the next day and Rita was still sleeping. I hit the block.

I hadn't seen or spoken to my dad or Satannie in about a year, but he reached out and told me he was now DJ'ing at the Chris Rock Show and invited me to come down. I was excited about going to the show. It was usually the only way I got to spend time with my dad so it wasn't too surprising that, that would be the next time I got to see him. Either way, I couldn't wait to see him and to show him my beautiful new girlfriend.

We got to the show, I told the security who I was, and they let me right in, laughing, telling me; "Damn yo face was I.D. enough you aint even need to pull out that license".

Once I'd passed my road test, I loved flashing my license.

The show hadn't started, and the seats were still all empty so, I got to see Chris Rock practicing his jokes on stage.

Chris Rock, by this time was a larger-than-life superstar but if I hadn't seen him on TV and knew who he was, I couldn't tell. It was like he wasn't impressed by his own celebrity. He interacted with everyone and was super cool.

He looked at me and said, "I know this guy's somehow related to Flash..." and went down a list with his arm on my shoulder "...who are you? A Brother?" I laughed saying "No." "Uncle, cousin that wants to borrow some money?" I laughed and said "Nah, that's my pops". He said, "Aww man, how many kids Flash got?!". I said "6". He said, "Cool man, so you gon be a DJ like your dad?". Then somebody called him before I could answer, and he had to go. As he was leaving, I said, "A rapper". He asked what my rap name was, and I said "JayFlo". He poked his lips out, nodded up and down, repeated JayFlo to himself, and he was gone. I took Rita with me to my dad's dressing room, but he was standing in the hallway surrounded by staff. He spotted me and put his finger up, signaling me to give him a minute. When he was done, he ran over to me excited giving me a big hug, then looked at Rita, looked her up and down, put his arm around her and walked off while me and a few of his people followed a few steps behind.

I don't know what he was saying to Rita but, she was smiling and laughing. I didn't like it and it made me uncomfortable. I played it off like I wasn't bothered.

My father did something similar when I was in my early teens introducing him to a girl I liked, who also liked me named Kenyetta. It gave me the same feeling back then that it gave me at that moment.

He spoke to me a little bit then told me he had a job opportunity for me. He said he'd pay me $1000, and I said, "Cool what is it?". He said we'd talk more after the show, but we should get seated because it was about to start. Soon as he said that, the rapper "Mystikal" walked up to him and told him how it was an honor to meet him. Mystikal's song "Shake Ya Ass" was the hottest song on the radio at the time. My dad shook his hand and said, "Same here", then introduced me.

Mystical shook my hand and said, "What's up?". My dad rushed me and Rita off to our seats and Mystikal told me to come to his dressing room after the show so we could take a flick. I was hyped like "Hell yeah, definitely" and walked from the backstage area to our seats.

I looked to the left and these huge breasts in a spaghetti strapped dress caught my attention. I looked up at the face and it just so happened, she was staring at me. Rita elbows me softly and asks me if I knew her. I said, "No, that's the girl from the movie Love Jones". It was Lisa Nicole Carson.

Rita looked again and said, "Yeah, that is her. Well, why was she staring at you like that?". I said, "I don't know" and led her to our seats.

The show was awesome. My dad Intro'd, Chris joked, his guests spoke and Mystikal performed. Mystikal's dancers had on tight, shiny gold catsuits and they were very healthy looking. He killed it, and so did his dancers. The crowd was all in.

After the show, I found my dad and asked him what he was doing after the show. He invited us to come to a club he was DJ'ing, in lower Manhattan called Bentley's. I said "Cool", and looked back smiling at Rita but, she had a grimace, and her arms were folded. This had been the first time I'd brought a girl to anything like this. What she didn't understand was I've never been starstruck. Martin Luther King wasn't a mythical figure he was a man who made choices. Wer'e all just human beings. I learned that early.

-Chapter Eight-
The S.O.A.L. Survivor

Rita and I were at the end of our relationship. She just had way too much baggage, she was too insecure, jealous, physically and verbally abusive toward me and I took it for about a year. After a year of being beat on and talked down to I couldn't take it anymore. I decided to move on, and I immediately got focused on my plans.

I chilled with Jay in Hunts Point one day and we headed over to Satannie's house. My father was there. I hadn't seen him since the Chris Rock show the year before. He pretended to be concerned about me, but I was reluctant to lower my defenses around him. I didn't like him. I certainly didn't trust him anymore.

Days later Rita calls me and says, "I'm pregnant".

I said, "Pregnant? Since when?". She said, "I don't know, but we can go take a test if you don't believe me. I knew it was just a ploy to get whatever little time left she had to be in my presence. Rita already had a 3-year-old little girl named Jada that I adored. I said, "Okay in the morning, we gon go up to Bronx Lebanon and you can take the test there".

The next morning, we went to Bronx Lebanon on Fulton St., and I stayed outside, just thinking.

She came outside with the doctor; the doctor held the pregnancy test up and showed me. Sure enough, she was pregnant.

I fell flat on my back onto the concrete. The doctor helped me up and asked me if I was alright. I asked her if she could show me the stick one more time and explain to me how it works. She said, "Come inside, I'll explain to you both what to expect in the upcoming months and what you're going to need to do.

We left and headed over to Satannie's.

Now more than ever I needed to catch a lucky break. It was 2002, I was 26, expecting a son and I wasn't getting any younger.

I'd never stopped writing and with everything I'd gone through, I had a lot to say. The rapper 50 cent was blowing up and I'd heard he was making money touring just off a Mixtape.

I needed a Mixtape. I left my foot messenger job across the street from the World Trade Center at Deutsche Bank after the planes hit and was now working at Rite-Aid on Fordham Rd.

I wanted to get started on making my mixtape. Only problem. Where would I make this mixtape? I had no studio access, and I didn't make a whole lot of money. I kept working at Rite-Aid and stayed focused on making my Mixtape.

I called my father and told him Rita was pregnant hoping for some assistance or at least some advice. Neither happened.

I got introduced to an engineer named Triple-X down in the Lower East Side. He had a dope setup.

X turned his bedroom into a full-fledged studio and used his closet as the recording booth. We made our introductions, including his pitbull Red, and I got right to it. Time is money.

I was nervous, but I was ready. I'd written the whole mixtape to various beats, rehearsed and rehearsed 'til I had no need for my notebook, I had it all down packed. I freestyled the intro. I wanted that to be natural.

It had been almost 4 years since I'd been in the booth, it's how I know I have a gift from someplace special.

Whatever's inside me, it's always been there because it rose to the surface while I sat back and just let it take over. I ran through 10 songs in 4 hours. It was a 16 track Mixtape. I'd have to come back to finish the rest. I couldn't believe my ears.

After I left, I went to 96th st. in Manhattan to see my little brother Keith and his mother, Pam. I hadn't seen her in a long time, so we caught up with each other and I told her I was working on some music. I let her hear what I had so far, and she was super impressed.

So impressed, she believed I could make it. I told her it wasn't finished and to not tell my father what I was doing.

We talked about everything. She told me how she wanted another child, but she wanted my dad to be the father because she'd only given birth to my brother and wanted her children to have the same dad. I felt her on that. I knew I wasn't going to be like my father having a bunch of kids all over the place. I saw the effects of siblings living in separate households first-hand and the distance it created.

I told her I was expecting a baby from a girl I didn't want to be with, and she reminded me how, no matter what, I always needed to be there for my child because I knew exactly how it felt to grow up without a father. She knew she didn't have to remind me.

Pam loved and respected me. She always reminded me of how special I was and for that, I loved her right back. I told her, "Ma, trust me, I'll never leave my kid, I couldn't, it's not in me. No matter what, I'll give everything to make sure my kid turns out better than I did"/ "I know you will".

We chatted a little more and I headed out. As I was walking out Pam stopped me at the doorway and said, "I know music, even if your father doesn't want to help you, you're still his son. You're the son of a HIPHOP legend, and you're good. When your c.d.'s done, bring me a copy. I'm already in love with that one song

(Whereva We R), I like that one". I laughed and said, "Okay, I will", and headed out.

I went to the Lower East Side the next day to finish up my Mixtape and I'd written 1 more song the night before to let off my steam. The song "Let it out" was for my father.

I re-did my intro because, when I started the Mixtape, I got the idea to call it "Destroy and Rebuild" from my cousin Rahmel during one of his many God body lessons. I kept that title and added "The S.O.A.L. Survivor" because, when Pam called me the Son Of A HipHop Legend, I felt it. It put a meaningful stamp on me, and I ran with it. "The S.O.A.L. Survivor Vol. 1 Destroy and Rebuild". I got the Vol.1 part from Jay-Z's "In My Lifetime Vol.1".

My first Mixtape was done.

I'd already been scouting out places to duplicate my c.d. and settled on Media Outlet Solution on 135th St. in Harlem. I did a white label sticker with my name and the name of the c.d., it was wonderful. I could not contain my excitement.

I had 100 copies of my ideas, thoughts and creativity.

I took nothing and had made it into something.

As I was headed to the train station carrying my box, somebody stopped me and said, "Whatchu got their youngster?". A Harlem dude.

Harlem dudes are mad loud and are always talking about what they've got, whether it be; money, cars, clothes or anything of some sort of vanity.

My cousins from Harlem were no different. As I got older, I stopped looking at it as a bad thing. It's kind of what forced me to stay on my fresh and get money, just in case I came across a Harlem dude and had to defend myself. "What you sellin? C.d.'s? Who you got? Clue? Ron-G? Hurry up shorty I aint got all day"/ "Nah, this is me, this is my music?"/ "What? That's you? Fuck is you? Some sexy R&B singa? Fuck you do? Rap?"/ "Nah man, I rap. I just rap"/ "Aight, lemme hear some'm"/ "What? Right now?"/ "Yeah, right now. I wanna see what I'm buyin".

When he said "buying", I was like "Wow", in my head. I put the box down and I spit, "Done Talkin". As I was spittin, more people came. The more people came, the harder I went.

Before I could even finish, the dude cut me off saying "Aight shorty, don't give it aaall away". He yelled to the crowd that had gathered, "My man sellin his c.d., yall know he got it, he bout to blow up!". He leaned in and whispered, "What's your name?"/ "JayFlo"/ "Where you from?"/ "The Bronx"/ "My man JayFlo from the Boogie Down Bronx bout to sign his deal and you ca have it before it blows up! $5 a piece!!!". He reached in the box, and as he collected the money, he threw it into my box. When the crowd dispersed, I had $85.

I tried to give the dude some money, but he gave me $5 grabbed a c.d. and said, "Good luck, JayFlo from the Bronx", and walked off.

I'd taken nothing, turned it into something, and turned that, into money.

I headed home so I could put my c.d.'s in their individual cases in preparation of my sales.

I'd been taking good care of Rita throughout her pregnancy; Inever missed any pre-natal appts., gave her money, fed her, and we went to the movies, every single week. She'd stopped smoking weed and cigarettes like we agreed, and I was so proud of her holding things down while I was so busy making moves. We walked up the block to the park, sat there and just talked.

I asked her about her next appointment, and went to get something to eat, and I walked her back to the house. When I left her, I had 2 things on my mind: my car, and a better job. Oh yeah, and selling my c.d.'s, which wasn't going well.

I quickly figured out what the problem was with selling my cd's. One afternoon an episode of the Cosby Show that I'd seen plenty of times before, was being re-ran. Cliff Huxtable made an analogy, attempting to explain something to Vanessa.

He had her fiancé Dabnus Brickey imagine being served all his favorite foods, on a garbage can lid. It was a metaphor about "Presentation".

All my songs were great. Anyone who heard them, loved them, but I had a white sticker on c.d.'s, with black typing, in a clear vinyl case. I knew, I needed to step it up and take things seriously if I wanted to get in the game.

I'd kept this dope picture of my nephew Bishme and came up with the idea to use it for my album cover. This was it; I was stuck on using this picture. Only way I wasn't using it, is if Satannie told me I couldn't. I didn't want to call because I needed it too bad, so a couple weeks later I just went over to her house.

I knocked, she opened the door, saw it was me, said nothing and walked in the house. She didn't close it or lock it, so I assumed it was okay for me to come in.

Little Bishme saw me and immediately hopped up, caught me with a flying kick and ran off laughing. That shit hurt. I thought to myself; Damn, I'm getting old, how'd I let him catch me like that? He was about 4 years old at the time, but man was that a hard ass kick. I chased him and we started play fighting. After a little while, I knocked on Satannie's bedroom door, walked in and said what's up to big Bishme. We all started talking and stuff, and finally I decided to ask for what I came for. Bishme was cool with it instantly. I think Satannie was too, but she wanted me to sweat. I always felt she held resentment after I exposed her money triangle scheme.

She gave me the okay, I chilled a little bit longer, said bye to everybody, pushed my nephew to the floor and I was off.

I had the idea and knew what I wanted as far as my covers but had no idea how it worked, and it was too expensive to get my cover designed by the printing company so, I called the smartest person I knew; former D.D.T. member, my cousin Monroe. He knew exactly what to do so I sat back and watched him work.

He clicked this, copied that, colored here and when he called me in to the room to look... It was beautiful. My nephew in the center surrounded by my name and the Mixtape title gave it that official look I was hoping for. It was straight dope, but to me, it was missing something.

This was my product and I needed to give myself every advantage I could use to sell it.

In HipHop its this thing called a "Co-sign" and around this time it was becoming very popular. the "in" for the music business. All the top entertainers had one; 50Cent from Jam Master Jay, Eminem and Snoop from Dr. Dre and many others. I said "Monroe, type this in the bottom right-hand corner.

Son of the Legendary Grandmaster Flash".

He got hyped and said, "Oh hell yeah". It was done. I tried to pay him but, he wasn't having it so, we spoke a little longer and I left.

I got it pressed up in the new format and went to go see Pam in Manhattan. I showed her the prototype of the Mixtape and how it would look in its new format once the order was done.

Instead of a white label sticker, I got the title and my name lasered right on to the disc. She was so proud of me. We talked and she asked if my dad was going to help me get a deal. I said,

"No". She said, "Well did you talk to him about it?". I said, "Yeah, for years". We both laughed.

She said, "Well Im'a talk to him because he should be helping you". I chilled a little while longer playing with Keith. Cooking was never her favorite thing but whenever I came over, she'd whip up something, so I wasn't running on an empty stomach.

I was a grown man, and in a few months, I was going to be a father. I went out to Central Islip Long Island to my dad's house.

Most of the time whenever I stood right in front of my father, I felt like I wasn't standing there, like he couldn't see me.

As usual, he had to run and couldn't stay long. I just wanted to talk to him. I had so much on my mind; the baby, my Mixtape, Rita, just a lot. He didn't have time. It was what it was.

-Chapter Nine-

June 9th

The next day I went to Media Outlet Solution to pick up my discs and none other than the one and only; DJ Kay Slay was sitting in the back behind the counter. I didn't know much about him but once I heard his artist Papoose do a rap using the alphabets breaking down words with his lyrics, I became a fan of them both. I said what's up to him and told him I liked the song. He asked me if I rap and I said, "Yeah my names JayFlo". He said, "Alright", gave me a pound and got back to what he was doing. I didn't go hard promoting myself because I was sure people had done that with him all the time.

My order was done and this time, I didn't want to take the train, so I caught a cab. I put together one of my disc sets; c.d., the insert, the slim case and just marveled at it. Why hadn't I done it like this in the first place I thought.

I had a lot of the old c.d.'s left and decided I was going to give them away and sell the new ones. That's what I did, the very next day after work.

I went to Lower Manhattan, just going up to people making my pitch.

It was instant success.

I stopped just going up to people because now, people were coming up to me. People that were walking away were telling other people they'd just bought a c.d. from Grandmaster Flash's son. I was swarmed and surrounded, white people, young people, foreigners, male, and female.

I'd made one crucial mistake.

I only came out with about 20 c.d.'s. I had no clue they would go that fast. I sold all 20 c.d.'s in around 20 minutes for $5 a pop and left with $100. It took me almost 3 days to make that working at Rite-Aid. I knew 2 things at that moment; I wasn't going back to Rite-Aid, and I'd never run out of c.d.'s again.

I made so much money I was able to save up and purchased a vehicle all on my own. A 1996 champagne colored Toyota Camry.

I was mobile again. I started going borough to borough selling my c.d. I got so much love and support from people. With that dose of encouragement, I decided to go on the road, and I took Jay with me. We sold so many c.d.'s in Washington DC one time, I walked up to a dude, pitched my c.d. and he was like, "I already got it". I pulled out the c.d., showed it to him and confidently said, "Nah this JayFlo, you aint got this one".

He reached in his car window and pulled the c.d. out from his passenger seat. Me and Jay started laughing and yelled, "Ohhh!".

It felt good getting my name known while simultaneously getting paid. We grinded out all day and it got late so we headed back to the city.

I went to go see Satannie and when I got to the door, I heard my voice coming out of the apartment. I knocked and she let me in. I walked into the living room, and she was blasting my c.d. singing the lyrics to my song; "Azfasazucan!".

She had me rolling because she was going so hard. When the song was over, she was still in a zone breathing hard saying, "Wooh!".

I loved it. She told me everybody was talking about my c.d. "Nobody's talkin about nothin else".

My sister Satannie has this power over me that makes me feel 10ft. tall when she praises me, and the size of an ant when she puts me down. At that moment, I felt unstoppable.

I'd stopped by to give her an official copy of the c.d. plus Rita had a pre-natal appt. on the Grand Concourse, not too far from Satannie's house.

I had a lot of money saved up from selling my c.d. so I decided to put my hustle on hold.

The next few months, Rita and I spent every day together. We'd spent most of our time at Satannie's house. When we weren't there, we'd visit with someone else in the family.

Rita pregnant, was beautiful. Whenever I got a chance to look at her naked body with my child growing inside of it, I made slow, soft, careful love to it. Satannie decided to throw Rita a Baby Shower at her house, and it was awesome. All the family from all sides showed up. Even if they just came to drop a gift. When it was over, we had a ton of gifts and a couple bucks that would give us a nice start.

One day, I got a call from Rita, calmly telling me her water broke. I'd always thought when a woman's water broke, they were in pain, screaming, crying and going crazy. That's what I'd prepared myself for. I told her to stay still, and I was coming right away. She said, "I'm at the hospital already, my water broke while I was on the train". We'd agreed she wouldn't take the train for instances like this, but I wasn't about to bring it up. I zoomed up to Bronx Lebanon, rushed into the room and saw that Satannie was already there. Rita had an I.V. and had been prepped to have my son, then my aunt Penny walked in.

It was hours before Rita was set to start pushing. She'd waited too long from when they kept offering her the epidural, and now it was too late for her to get it. He was ready.

It looked like an exorcism. Rita was writhing in pain. Satannie and Penny sprang into action, even the doctors got out of their way. They coached her, rubbed her, squeezed cold rags on her face and did whatever it took, while I stood back, useless.

His head started coming out and the doctors stepped in. I couldn't believe what I was witnessing. I saw his face come out and the doctor quickly stuck something in his nose and mouth, sucking out fluid, next came his shoulders then he started crying. The rest of his body just slid and popped right out then they started cleaning him off. They put 2 white clips on the cord and told me to cut it. Probably the only useful thing I did.

Had Penny and Satannie not been there, that may have gon worse for me, than it did for Rita. I went over to her.

I looked over to see Satannie crying tears of joy, Penny's eyes locked on the baby and Rita looking completely exhausted. I held her hand, rubbing her hair thinking to myself; Damn, I'm only a man.

Satannie was the first family that got to hold him because Rita was so wiped out, she hadn't opened her eyes to look down at the baby the doctor layed on her chest, so Satannie picked him up, then Penny, then the doctors took him off. I was scared. Rita hadn't sprung back to herself yet and I began to worry. The West Indian nurse in her accent said, "She's fine dad don't worry. She just needs a little rest".

I stayed with Rita until she woke up. Satannie had already left to get back to get Jada and her kids. Penny gave her a ride.

Joseph Saddler III was 7lbs. 15oz. born June 9, 2003 @ 9:27pm. Peace, born into a world full of chaos. I had to protect him. I had to be there always to defend him. As I fed him his bottle, I saw the world in his little face. I was instantly infatuated with him, his little fist gripped around my one finger. I looked over at his mother lying back in the hospital bed, blank staring at the ceiling and said to her, "It's gonna be okay, everything's gonna be alright". I would've given anything to know exactly what was on her mind at that moment.

I came back every day until it was time for her to leave. My aunt Barbara, my mom, my sisters and a bunch of people visited steadily during her stay to come see the newest addition to our clan. When it was time to leave, the doctor said we couldn't leave without a car seat. Unbeknownst to me, my aunt Barbara already had it covered and presented it to the doctors. It was time to go.

My family would visit to congratulate us and bring more gifts for the baby. We didn't have much as far as furniture, so I knew I had to get back on my grind. I hadn't lost that itch to be on, and it was about time I started scratching it again.

I'd previously been selling my c.d. so successfully that I got a call from my father asking me, "Why are you selling a c.d. with my name on it?". I hadn't seen or spoke to my father since I came out to Long Island and he had to rush off. I tried to lighten the situation by saying, "Well, you do know that you have a new grandson, right?".

He started yelling at the top of his lungs "Take my name off the c.d. Joe!". I tried to explain to him, that it's what was gaining peoples interest, and if I took it off it wouldn't be as easy to sell. He screamed, "I don't care Joe! Take my fucking name off the c.d.!!!". I told him, "I'm not gonna do that, it doesn't make any sense". I tried to further explain but he just hung up the phone.

I called Penny to tell her what happened, and she said, "It's that song JoeJoe! Ever since Pam played it for him, he will not stop talking about it, he's embarrassed!".

The song she was referring to was "Let it out". I said, "He wants me to take his name off the c.d". She said, "Tuh, well then, he needs to help you. You're his son! I just don't get Butsy", (as his sisters called him). I said to her "I didn't have his name on the c.d. at first and it barely sold. Soon as I put his name on it, I couldn't keep enough.". She said, "Well fuck him then. You do what you gotta do for you and yours, has he seen the baby?"/

"No"/ "Well what did he say about him?"/ "Nothing". She said, "Well tuh, you do what you gotta do. I love you Pop and don't worry about it, I'm proud of you and you gon be okay. Kiss that baby for me"/ "I will Auntie, love you too".

I wasn't mad Pam played the song. I knew eventually he'd hear it. I feel like, it made him angrier to hear it through Pam because, unlike his 3 other baby mothers, Pam forced him to take care of my brother Keith. She was no joke; she took legal action and he had to pay. He hated it.

I called Satannie because she always spoke to him and from what she told me, it was an old acquaintance of his I didn't know, that complimented him on how dope I was. After that, he heard the song when he visited Pam and was livid.

I kept selling the c.d. as it was.

We had good times as a family. The baby brought us so much joy. I loved being a dad. I'd even drink Rita's breast milk straight from her breast.

I'd gotten the support I needed and made it through the roadblocks to arrive at the demands of a second disc. I'd heard a lot of people saying that year, "Charge it to the game", whenever certain things happened. My first Mixtape made a lot of things happen. Good and bad. It wasn't a game to me so, in 2003, I named my 2nd Mixtape "S.O.A.L. Survivor Vol.2 Charge it to the Grind", got my instrumentals together and started writing.

Being a new father was a struggle and multi-tasking, putting in the groundwork to become a potential HIPHOP star didn't make it easier.

My whole life I wanted to be a rapper, but it wasn't all I wanted. I wanted love. I wanted a family. One without the other and the dream would be incomplete.

I finished my Mixtape, flew through it and headed back home. Lil Joe was going to be a year old, and I wanted to do something special for him, so I invited the family over and Rita cooked this huge dinner; her first time doing such a thing, from what she told me. Everyone showed up, including my dad. We all celebrated Joe's being a year old and partied hard.

I caught Satannie's eye across the living room and she was waving me in to come toward her. I told Rita I'd be right back and walked over to her. She grabbed my hand and I followed. She found my dad in the kitchen, grabbed his hand, walked us out into the hallway, said, "Talk", and walked back inside the house.

It was awkward.

***

Satannie had, when she and I were small children gotten to a point where she was fedup with my dad's crap too and called his home phone but, he didn't answer. She left a message on his answering service of the song by HipHop group Ed O.G. & the Bulldogs "Be a father to your child".

She couldn't have been older than ten and was already bold. Years later he denied Satannie was his daughter and as a full-grown adult forced her into court to take a paternity test. Results showed what anyone with even the worst eyesight knew. He was the father.

***

My father said, "So how you been?"/ "Good, might be startin a new job pretty soon"/ "Cool, I might have a job I need you to do". I'd never stopped writing, but I'd given up on making it in the music industry. He told me he was working on a project for Microsoft called; "The 5.1 Project" and wanted me to write a song for it. He said 5.1 was the wave of the future, and if I did it,

I'd be the first artist in history to do so. He offered to pay me upfront and said I'd also receive writer's royalties.

I told him I'd think about it and get back to him. He said, "Okay, well I have a session coming up soon, if you're in, meet me downtown at Quad studios" and gave me a card with the address on it.

I went for my job interview with Grand Prix. I filled out the application on a whim. I'd filled out a lot of applications. I never thought they'd be the ones to call me back because I had no experience as a driving instructor. I was glad they did. I took all the tests, drug, a written and a special road test for instructors in training.

I got my first student in July. I was nervous as hell, but I did awesome. I got my first check, and it wasn't much, but I only had a couple students so far.

I got back to business and decided to do the song for my father, "Go Flash!" is the worst song I've ever recorded. I didn't think anything could top "Over Here Over There" but, this bumped it out the top spot. My father made the beat, paid me $1000.

After the song was done, he invited me to Miami for a meeting with the Microsoft people about the project.

I never got to meet with the Microsoft people except one guy, who's name escapes me but, my father says the guy in charge of the project ended up having a baby, got married and things were going to be put on hold. I never heard another word about the project, or my song. My dad told me not to worry about it and offered me another opportunity.

He told me he was going on a European tour wanted me to join him, and I should consider signing to his label as his premier artist. He told me to get a lawyer and we'd work out the details later. For now, he'd be taking me across seas to get my feet wet. I agreed, with no intentions of signing anything because, I didn't trust him, but why turn down a chance to enhance my skills and get a bigger fan base.

He said he'd pay me $400 for each trip. I still had Grand Prix, and as a driving instructor I made my own schedule so, I booked around the Tour dates. My father got my Passport expedited, and we were off.

It was cool getting to be around my dad and I appreciated him inviting me on his tour and began to reconsider signing with him. I tried to speak to him about a few things I didn't understand in the contract, but he would have none of it. He wanted to speak about no part of the contract and told me to let the lawyers deal with it. I let it go, as a matter of fact my dad didn't really speak to me at all. Besides the performances, we never spoke. He just stayed in his room. First place we stopped was Norway.

We stayed at this place that looked like one of those castles in the movies; dark, dreary and gray, but still fancy. We settled in and got prepared to hit the set because we had another show immediately following, in a town called Oslo. Demo and I served as my dad's hype-men in the first show. I bombed.

I had little, to no skills as a showman. I'd blazed plenty of booths and sold many c.d.'s, but at 27, had minimal physical performances under my belt besides rhyming in cyphers, performing at the Pyramid in lower Manhattan, and club Nell's. I'd never even shot a video. I got stuck during the set and said "Yo, yo, yo" like 20 times in a row. My father cleaned it up and saved the show. I was totally embarrassed. My Dad and Demo told me not to worry about it, and it happens to everybody. They had a good laugh snapping on me about it on the way to the next show though. My dad was dying laughing, saying, "I think you just said the most Yo's in rap history". Me and Demo started laughing.

We got to the next show and this time, my dad gave me a couple of tips before I went on, so I'd do better than the previous time. This crowd was a little bigger than the last, but I did a lot better and me and Demo were a lot more in sync, covering the stage. Next stop, Paris. We stayed at a luxurious hotel just across from "The Moulin Rouge". The staff told me the hotel we were staying in was the singer, Prince's favorite place to stay when he was in Paris. We checked in, headed to our rooms, and when I got to mine, I got a phone call.

My dad was married to Felicia by this time and when I answered the phone, surprisingly it was her. I was surprised because, we never spoke except for a couple of times.

She told me that Ashton Kutcher's show "Punk'd" reached out to her, wanted to punk my dad, and they needed my help. They were going to give me crates that looked exactly like the crates he carried his records in.

Whenever we finished a show, Me and Demo pushed the crates outside to load them into the car. My dad had five crates, each one a different color and looked like huge treasure chests.

He even named them after Me and my siblings.

They wanted me to "Accidentally" leave the replica crates in the street by the curb and a car would come by, crashing the crates. I knew instantly I wanted no part of that prank.

I know how my dad feels about his records and knew he wouldn't find it funny. At all. Joke or no joke. I told her I'd pass, but I got a great chuckle off the thought.

We had one more stop in Cannes, then the city Nice and then we were going back to the states for a couple of days before we had to be in Holland.

-Chapter Ten-

<u>Def Jam</u>

I got back home, and Rita was so excited to see me. Joe and Jada ran up to my leg while Rita and I just looked at each other smiling. I greeted Rita as she continued to do the dishes. I walked up behind her kissing on her ears, rubbing on her stomach as she reached her soapy hands back and started rubbing my head.

I turned the water off, put Jada and Joe in front of the TV with cartoons and snacks, took her in the room and licked every part of her sexy body. Rita'd started complaining that she'd gotten fat after the baby. To me, she gained weight in all the right places, and any part of her body she complained about, I gave extra special attention.

Afterwards, she lit up her blunt and I shared stories about my "Rock Star" life. Her first question, "And... what about the girls?". I just told her the truth; "Even if I wanted to do something I couldn't, my father was too much on top of me and Demo. He kept us busy always doing something, and we never stayed anywhere long enough to meet any girls. We'd set up, do a show, pack up, back to the hotel, sleep, board the plane and repeat". Her only response was, "Mmmhmm".

I decided the next time we went out I was gonna bring copies of my Mixtapes, so I got them replicated.

Amsterdam was my favorite place. Everybody was so nice. We stayed at a hotel that was close to the "Red Light District". There, women were inside a building facing the street, in their own private windows, on display wearing only sexy negligee's, ready to trade sex for money, and it was legal. They also had trucks parked along the side of the street with fully furnished bedrooms in them to have sex for a fee.

I was raised in Hunts Point and learned early "Only Tricks pay for pussy". Up the block they also had a store that sold all kinds of weed. This was also legal. It was amazing to see people walking around in public, smoking weed right in front of the police. I'd figured out why everyone was so very nice.

Next door to the hotel was a boutique with exclusive Hilfiger gear. Andy Hilfiger was there and knew who my father was. He liked me and asked if I would wear his clothes for the show. I'd earlier put it together why rich and famous people were given things for free, marketing and advertising. If a famous person wore their product, that famous person's fans would then go buy what they saw that famous person wearing. It was business. Good business.

I turned it down so I didn't seem greedy but, he insisted, and my father told me it would be considered rude, so I accepted. He told me I could pick whatever I wanted. I picked a couple of outfits, thanked him and told him it was a pleasure meeting him.

I got back to the hotel and sat in the lobby waiting for my dad to come back in. I wasn't sure where Demo was, but I didn't want to go back upstairs by myself.

It was showtime. This time, I killed it. I asked my dad if at the next show, I could get a few minutes to do one of my songs. I'd shown him I was a fast learner so; I just took a shot. He said yes.

As we were getting into the last song on the set, the rapper Coolio walked out on to the stage. I couldn't believe it! I was onstage performing with Coolio. I passed him the mic, when he finished, he passed it back. When we finished, I bowed down to him, he instantly and gracefully bowed right back down to me, then we bowed to the audience and walked off stage. When we got backstage, I fell flat on my back. Everybody rushed over to me, to make sure I was okay.

I stared straight up at the ceiling lying on my back with a big cheese on my face and said, "I just performed with Coolio". Everybody laughed, smacking me in my head telling me to get up and how I'd scared them. Next stop; Winchester London.

We got to the U.K., where everything was opposite for me. The steering wheels were on the opposite side and so was the road. People drove crazy with their tiny vehicles swerving and slashing through traffic, bending corners at high speeds as if driving safely was an abnormal occurrence. New York City driving had nothing on these people.

We got to the hotel and Demo started talking to this guy sitting in the lobby. I didn't recognize him until Demo came and told me it was the singer, Mario. He had the hit song "Just a friend" and was promoting his new single "Let Me Love You". He looked like a street dude, white Doo-rag and a red hoody. He had a good vibe about him. We got upstairs and this big, tall white dude was assigned to me, as my security/escort. I didn't understand why I needed security. Nobody even knew who I was.

My father told me to go get dressed because I was going to be getting interviewed, and they wanted to take pictures of me. I got fresh to death in my green and white Boston Celtics bucket, green and white Tim's, my free Hilfiger jeans, green and white Girbaud shirt, got down to the lobby and it was go time.

My dad rode with his escort in a separate car, while I rode with my escort and Demo. Wherever it was, I don't remember but there were a lot of celebs there. I could barely see because as soon as I stepped out, I was blinded by the cameras flashing in my face. My escort walked me in, and I saw a huge banner that read "Homelands".

He walked me down the red carpet to an area that had a big wall with MTV logo's all over it.

The photographers called out "JayFlo, over here!" and blinded me with the flash. They kept calling me, so I kept turning my head giving them the best HIPHOP faces, stances and poses I grew to have naturally. I was still blinded and could only hear.

As I posed for the pictures, I heard my dad's voice on the side of me, eerily saying things like, "Is this what you want? You ready to be a star? This is what it is Joe. You ready for this life?" all while the cameras were flashing. He sounded like a Demon to me. He'd killed the fun. I just ice grilled him and walked off.

The escort took me off to an area where I got interviewed. I answered a couple questions and let them know my relationship with HipHop, but my mood was blown so I just cut it short.

Tim Westwood walked up to my dad and started to talk to him. My dad introduced me, but Tim gave me a half-hearted "Hey" and kept talking to my dad.

It was almost time for us to go on. At that moment, as I stood stage left, Dizzee Rascal was onstage, and the crowd was going crazy for him "Fix up, look sharp" was all I could make out of this rapid spitting London based rapper. I barely understood anything he was saying, but that's the thing with music; when it's good, your soul knows. I was afraid because we'd be up to perform soon, and my dad picked up on it.

There were 30,000 people in the crowd. So far, the most I'd performed in front of was about 5,000. My dad said, "Whatever you put out to them, that's what you're gonna get back. Give them a lot of energy, you'll get it right back. Give them a little, same thing. You're the MC, the master, don't forget it". It was time. Right then, I drifted off and let whatever that thing is inside of me take over and... Boom! I was off.

I covered that huge stage like it was 3 of me. My dad on the wheels of steel behind me, and Demo at my side gave me the confidence I needed. DJ Jazzy Jeff snuck up on the stage, sat behind my pops and had the best seat for the rest of the set. My pops taught me a lot of "Call and Response" techniques, so I had the crowd under my control.

Halfway through the set, it was time for my 2-song solo performance. I could barely hear myself, but the reaction of the crowd let me know I was on point.

I handed the show back over to my dad like a well ran relay. He paused the show with a magical slow-down of the record he was spinning so he could make an announcement.

He said, "Winchester! What's!! Uuuuup??!!!", as the crowd went crazy, he casually walked down from behind his turntable and waved for me to meet him center stage, put his arm around me then said, "Winchester! I'd like to introduce you to JayFlo; the first artist on my new label Adrenaline City Entertainment...". The crowd went crazy, cheering and clapping. He continued "... JayFlo is not only special because he's my first artist! ... He's also, my sonnn!".

The crowd cheered so loud it went silent, that's what I remember. Then the sound came back. After the announcement, my father got back in position, and we finished the set. Demo, my father and I walked centerstage, joined hands and took a bow.

As we walked off to head backstage, all I heard was chants from the crowd saying, "JayFlo, JayFlo, JayFlo", repeating it over and again. It was completely weird, and totally overwhelming. Everybody backstage was just staring at me.

When I finally met my father's eyes, they were out of place. In a room full of admiration and congrats toward me, my father's demeanor was puzzling. He hadn't said anything to me since we'd left the stage.

It had all been because of him, without him, no one would've even cared who I was. He'd made everything possible, and I needed his input desperately. I waited for him to say something, anything. We made it back to the hotel and still, nothing.

I asked Demo what he thinks my pops thought and he said, "You killed it"/ "My dad's not saying anything"/ "Don't sweat it, your pops has his ways but, you did good, and everybody knows that". I ordered some food and watched TV while Demo talked on the phone. My dad, as usual stayed in his room all night.

The next day it was time to check out and head back to the states. I met Demo already sitting downstairs with his luggage in the lobby. My dad called me up to the desk and all I could think was finally, he's gonna say something. He says, "Look at this", and slides a sheet of paper in front of me.

It was an added charge of $400.00 for a phone call that was made from my room. I was like, "Daaang. That's only one phone call?". My dad, with a dead serious face says, "Yes Joe, it's an international call, who's supposed to pay for this?". I never used the phones, so I called Demo over and said to him, "Yo, that call you made was $400.00". My father said, "Sit down Demo". Demo said nothing, went and sat down.

My dad said, "You let Demo make the call from your room, you're responsible for the bill".

All I was expected to get was $400.00, so basically, he wanted me to go home with nothing. I kept calm, said nothing and walked off, but I was boiling.

We got to the airport and on a layover somewhere, Fatman Scoops brother; Young Sav, was seated not too far from me. I introduced myself and we started talking. I gave him a copy of my c.d., and as we walked through the terminal, I noticed Funkmaster Flex and stopped to talk to him. I told him about my c.d., but I didn't have any left. I remembered that I gave Demo a c.d., so I ran over to Demo and promised I'd give him one when we got back to America.

Demo gave me the disc but, as I'm running back over to where Funkmaster Flex is standing, my dad popped up out of nowhere, snatched the disc out of my hand like an interception and walked back over to where our party was waiting. I glanced back at Flex, he met my eye and stood there. I just walked away.

We got to LaGuardia Airport, and I lost it. My father was still talking about not paying me and his treatment of me was altogether intolerable. I was not going home with no money.

On the ride to his house, everyone felt the tension between us, but these were my father's yes-men, and woman, his manager Blue. When we pulled up to his house, I handled the situation, the same way I would, where somebody doesn't want to give me something I'm owed, The wrong way. I took my jewelry off way in the backseat of the 4-row van, while noticing my dad take his jewelry off in the front passenger seat. We got to the front of his Long Island home, both hopped out and everybody got right in between us.

I calmly asked him, over everyones shoulders, "Are you gonna pay me my money?". He calmly went into his suitcase, pulled out his checkbook, wrote me a check for $400 and said, "You're off the tour. I couldn't believe this was really happening. I couldn't believe it! After that amazing performance I'd put on in London? I said, "What?! Off the tour?!". My father said nothing else. I said a whole lot as he offered me his back heading into his house, and I ended it with, "Fuck You!". I didn't care at that moment. I grabbed my suitcase, turned around, and walked from his house, all the way to the L.I.R.R.

The train ride helped it all to sink in. It really hit me. Hours before, I was JayFlo, adored by tens of thousands. Hours later, I was JoeJoe, headed uptown on the 2 train.

I still had my job at Grand Prix so, I wasn't totally screwed. I got home to my family, sunk myself into them and forgot all about London, plus I had a couple dollars so, we were good.

I was a little depressed about the way things went down with my dad but, he re-lit a fuse in me that had went out. I'd let the thought of me getting on in the music industry go.

Seeing, and feeling the support of the people, knowing I can do what I love and make a living while supporting my family, made it an easy decision.

I kept working at Grand Prix and kept selling my c.d.

One day I was downtown, and the thought just hit me.

Without hesitation, I acted on my thought.

I went on 50th St. in lower Manhattan to the building I knew to be Def Jam and walked in.

***

In my teens, DJ AJ Scratch (S.I.P.) took me personally, to Lyor Cohens office.

I rapped for him, and he liked me, but all Lyor would talk about was this guy; Jay-Z.

He asked if I'd heard of him, what I thought of him and had I heard his song; "Aint No N***a". My meeting was more about this other rapper than it was about me. He turned me down, told me to keep working, and his door was always open to me.

***

This time, I entered the building through the deliveries entrance and pretended to be a foot messenger. I knew the procedure from being a foot messenger years before at Madison Square Garden. I got inside, made it to the elevator and a man stopped me, "Yo!".

I jumped startled, turned around discouraged and said, "Yeah?". He said, "You can't go up there without this", gave me a sticker badge and I was on my way. I got upstairs, got off the elevator to this grimy looking area and walked down the hall. I saw this big door at the other end so, I walked down and opened it.

The other side had this huge glamorous office space; Def Jam, I'd made it. I knew time was limited so I tried to look for anyone who could help me, anyone who looked familiar. I pushed open door after door saying "Sorry, wrong office".

As I kept walking, I saw a silver haired chubby white guy coming down the hall, who looked like a security officer, and he saw me, so I dipped into the office closest to me. It was occupied by about 8 black young, hood looking dudes.

It just so happens, it was Roc-a-Fella CEO, Dame Dash's office. One of the dudes looked at me and said, "Yo, who the fuck is you?". The dude, who I'd later find out's name, was Ramses. I just told the truth, "My name is JayFlo this is my c.d., I want a record deal".

Everybody just paused, looked at each other, looked back at me, then busted out laughing.

Through the laughter there was a knock on the door. That security guard.

He looked at me, then looked at Ramses and said, "How you doin sir? Everything alright?". He called the security guard by name and told him, "Yeah, everything's alright", and the guard closed the door.

Ramses snatches the c.d. out of my hand and said, "Okay, spit". I said, "But, my disc, I got mad music on there"/ "I understand that, spit, or you can leave my office. You want a deal? This is what you gotta do. You go up to Cam (Killa Cam) or anybody they gon tell you the same thing. If ya shit is garbage they won't even listen to your c.d, it's goin straight out the window. Spit.".

I don't know if it was me or Freeway who first asked that dumb ass question, "Can I get a beat?" but, Ramses answer was the same as Swizz Beats, "Nah, no beat"/ "Aight, Fuck it".

I just started spittin. As I was spittin, their reactions couldn't hide how dope they thought I was, I was feelin myself. Feeling myself right up until I got to the end of my verse and the dude immediately started spittin right after me trying to show me how dope my verse wasn't.

The crowd was hype off the fact that he started spittin. "Get em Vein! Get em!".

Vein Lane. I tagged in at the end of his verse like it was planned. "Uh-oh, what do we have heeere!", I heard in the background. I gave all I had. The more I gave, the more Vein forced me to give. We went back and forth until Ramses stopped it.

They all gave me props and Ramses promised to listen to my c.d.

I headed back downstairs and something else dawned on me.

As I exited the message center, I walked up to the mail clerk and said, "Yo, yall get Lyor Cohen's mail down here don't yall?"/ "Yes sir, I deliver it to him personally"/ "So, if I give you this c.d., you'll make sure he gets it?"/ "Yes sir, I most certainly will"/ "Okay, cool, and here's one for you". He looked at the cover and said, "Word? Yo, so how's your dad these days?"/ "Well, very well. He's touring and just started his own record label"/ "Alright JayFlo, I'll make sure Mr. Cohen gets this man, good luck"/ "Thanks, I appreciate it".

I couldn't believe all that had happened. I took a chance, stepped up and it paid off. I was so excited, I got home and told Rita all about it.

Later that night, the house phone rings. Rita, in the kitchen answers it and says "Hello?"/ "Hey Rita, it's Flash let me speak to Joe". Rita jokingly says, "Well hello to you too sir". Then in that shrill, seering, sonically fluid, annoying tone I'd come to love, Rita yells, "Jooooee! Phoooonnne!!".

I walk into the kitchen and calmly say, "You know I'm only in the next room, right?", she laughs and hands me the phone.

I say, "Hello?".

In a smiling, laughing tone, He says, "Hey Joe, heard you stopped by Def Jam today"/ "Pops?".

Shocked to hear from him, I continued excitedly, "What's up Pops? Yeah, I was dropping my c.d. off, but bust how I got into the building though…". Proud of myself, about to tell him my story, he cut me off and said, "Since you won't listen to me, I'm gonna let you hear it from the man himself", and hands the phone off.

The voice said,

"Hello?…".

I hadn't at that second caught on to the part where my dad said, "Since you won't listen to me" and was slightly excited that I was about to hear some good news,

"…Yeah, is this Joe Jr.?". I exhuberantly replied, "Yezzirrr"/ "Yeah, this is Lyor Cohen. I'm here with your dad and umm, I don't know what's going on between you guys, but you've really got to work it out before we can do any business"/ "But, I do my own thing, no one has any holds over me"/ "I understand that, and I respect what you do, but your father and I have been friends for over 20 years and, I just wouldn't want to disrespect that"/ "Well, did you listen to my c.d.?"/ "No, not yet but, keep doing what you're doing, my door is always open to you. Work out everything with your dad and who knows, but right now, I gotta go Joe, hope to talk to you soon". I sorrowfully said, "Alright man".

My father got back on the phone immediately monolouging, "And that's how it goes Joe. You want in this business it's through me, if not, you get out in the streets build your own name and do battle just like I had to do. I built me, and my group! Get your name known on your own and start making music people wanna hear Joe! That street shit is played out. I told you years ago, you gotta make stupid songs. The average consumer is stupid and doesn't want to think after a hard day's work. If you want in, I'm the door, now, I gotta go do this party, talk to you soon (click)".

I was stuck, holding the phone, listening to the tone. The garbage was full, which reminded me that Rita had already asked me a few times to take it out. Lil Joe was at the kitchen table falling asleep, Jada was eating a slice of pizza, and the Malcolm, Nelson and Martin painting we had hanging on the wall drew me in as I thought to myself, why? Why, out of all the people on this planet called earth, God had to make Grandmaster Flash my father.

The phones busy signal snapped me out of my trance.

I felt, with my father's actions, he wanted to keep me hid.

My new album "The Best Kept Secret", was recorded in Hunts Point, next door from my old apartment, at my man Verse's crib. Verse had a dope sound. He was from Brooklyn but moved to the Bronx to raise his newborn baby with his wife. The album had all original beats, and after writing to all the beats, it took us just 3 days to record it.

The album was dope but, with no plan, no support and most importantly, no money to promote it, I guess it really would be a secret, and that's how it stayed.

I started going harder at my job, picking up new students. Anybody they threw me, I'd put them on my calendar, instead of turning them down like before. Once I got a $1000 check, for 5 days of just sitting in a car telling people what to do, I was off and running. This is how I was gonna get the money I needed I thought to myself. I might not have got to go hard with the last album I recorded but I was already writing for my new album and had new ideas on how I was gonna promote it.

The following year I recorded "Trial and Error". It took about 5 weeks.

The last album I recorded "The Best Kept Secret", had samples on every song. I'd heard about the negative effects samples can have on a record, how it can cause setbacks, and become expensive even though it helps fans catch on quicker. Trial and Error had 16 songs and 1 sample on one song. I had a problem with the sample, but I figured I'd cross that bridge when I got to it.

This was my first official album. It had a bar code, a booklet, graphic art on the c.d. and the album was shrinkwrapped.

I got it pressed up immediately and started selling it in the streets of Atlanta where HipHop was beginning to dominate.

I posted up in the parking lot at a club in Georgia one night called "Club Chocolate". On this night, T.I. was performing, and a few of his people were standing outside in the parking lot. They saw me selling my c.d. in the crowd and asked me what I was doing. I started pitching to him in the same fashion I'd do with any potential purchaser. He bought 5 c.d.'s and gave me a crispy $100 bill. I tried to give him his change, but he stopped me and said, "Naw, that's fa you shawty, keep hustling". My c.d.'s were $10 a pop, so basically, he bought 5 c.d.'s and just gave me 50 bucks.

I caught a light bulb, I needed to get back home. Fuck it. It's now or never. I was determined to be heard.

Somebody was giving me a deal.

-Chapter Eleven-
April 12th

I got back home and got on my grind immediately. I sold my new disc for $10, as opposed to my Mixtape, which I'd been selling for $5. Once people saw I had a professional disc that looked just like the ones in the record stores, they gave up the $10, as quickly as they had with my Mixtape when my fathers name was on the front.

This time, it was all me.

I sold close to 1200 copies hand to hand over the next couple months. For the 3rd time, I was headed back to Def Jam.

This time, Lyor Cohen was working for another label and Jay-Z was now the president of Def Jam. I got upstairs with ease using the same format, through the messenger's entrance.

Def Jam had gotten a lot of upgrades since the last time I was there and looked way snazzier.

Once I passed the huge frames of artists like DMX and Ja-Rule, I got to the offices.

Within minutes, I spotted Jay-Z's right-hand man Ty-Ty sitting in an office having what looked like was a business meeting with 2 females.

I poked my head in and said, "Sorry to interrupt. My name is JayFlo, I was just handin out my new c.d.". He said, "JayFlo? Alright JayFlo and just how the fuck did you get in here?"/ "Oh nah, it's cool, I just wanted to give you this and be on my way". He got up from behind his desk, walked passed me out into the hallway and asked again, this time to everyone within earshot "How the fuck! Did he get in here?!! This is the number 1 label, with the number 1 artist! How the fuck did he get in here?!!". He was flippin.

He looked at me, snatched the c.d. and said, "Gimme this shit, I aint even mad at you, it's not your fault", and walked back into his office.

I went back to the elevator and as I stood there and waited, a security guard and a police officer walked up behind me and just stood there, waiting with me for the elevator to come.

They rode down with me without saying a word. They followed me off, handed me a sheet of paper and told me, if I didn't sign it, I would be arrested on the spot.

I read it, signed it, and they led me out of the building.

The paper stated, I was banned from the building for 1 year. If I even stood on the same block as Def Jam, I'd be arrested.

I went from confident to discouraged in a matter of minutes and rode a depressing train ride home.

Trial and Error was the name of my album and the best way I could describe the life I was living.

Around this time, I got a call from my brother Keith, which was strange because, he'd never called me before. I'd always called or visited Pam and that was how he and I stayed connected. When he told me, something was wrong with Pam and she was in the hospital, I shot right up. I got Lil JoeJoe and myself dressed and headed to the hospital.

When I got to the hospital, I sat in the lobby for about a half an hour. Pain was upstairs, waiting, I knew it, I felt it. I got upstairs and waited in the hallway another 20 minutes. Keith's sadness over the phone gave me a feeling that it was something serious, but I rushed off before asking anything.

Before I could make it into the room, Nina spotted me and called my name. I looked at her and put my head down. She came over, hugged me tight and held on. In our embrace, I asked, "Is she gonna be, okay?". She released me, with no eye contact wiping her running nose and said, "I don't know JoeJoe, it doesn't look good". Through my welling eyes I asked her, "What happened?"/ "The doctors said she had an Aneurysm. She was at home with Swan, and he rushed her over here. They did an emergency Tracheotomy, and she's on a breathing machine"/ "What?!!, Nina."/ "Yeah Joe, it's bad". She took my hand to go inside, but I told her to give me a minute and I'd be in. She said okay and walked inside.

I waited a few minutes and walked in, Lil JoeJoe following behind. I looked at Pam. Pam's always been very light skinned. She resembled to me, the singer Sade. Laying there, she was pale, her eyes were closed, sunken in, and she wasn't moving. I walked over to Pams mother Ms. Howell, gave her a hug and introduced her to Lil JoeJoe. I thought to myself how she'd already lost her son Kevin, and Pam needed to pull through this, for her mother's sake. I grabbed Pam's hand and called to her, "Ma, ma, Pam, it's me JoeJoe, I'm here". As hard as I tried not to, I put my head on her hand and started crying. Nina and Ms. Howell came over rubbing my back, and by the time I'd gotten up, Nina was handing me tissues while wiping her own nose. Ms. Howell was just telling me, "It's gonna be alright", comforting me, when it should've been the other way around. She didn't need it. She was the strongest person in the room. Talking to Pam as if she was wide awake, wiping the excess saliva from Pammy's face, as she fondly called her daughter.

I stepped out of the room to get some air, gather my thoughts, went to the cafeteria and bumped into Swan. I could tell he was still in some sort of shock so, I tried to offer him some of that comfort Ms. Howell offered to me, by telling him how Pam spoke highly, regarding him. We spoke a little and after a while, I went back into Pam's hospital room. I stayed a little while longer, spoke to her, held her hand and told her I would be back to see her. I couldn't take it anymore. I hugged Ms. Howell, Nina, gave Pam a kiss, grabbed Joe's hand and headed out the room to leave. Halfway to the door, an almost 3year old JoeJoe pulled away from me, ran back and hugged the corner of Pam's hospital bed. You see? That's exactly what I mean about him. Pam had only seen JoeJoe a few times when he was a baby, but he felt the energy in the room, and showed everybody just how large of a heart he was carrying in that small body.

The next time I went to see Pam, she hadn't gotten any better. I talked to her then started talking to Ms. Howell. I saw Pam when I looked in her face and heard Pam's voice in her speech. Nina was there, and Shari, Pam's older sister. As the conversation went on, it seemed personal, so I left and went to the cafeteria. When I came back, I was ready to go. Nina told me the doctors weren't giving good news about Pam's condition. They had no hope of her recovering and felt the family should prepare to pull the plug. I was devastated. I walked into the room, gave Ms. Howell a hug and she asked if I was leaving. I sighed, "Yeah" and she had that same supportive face saying, "Okay, well, come back, I'm sure Pammy will be glad to see you". I said nothing. I went over to Pam, put my forehead to the side of her face, whispered, "Thank you, I love you", kissed her cheek, and said "Goodbye". I'd had enough. All I could do at that point was hope for the best. The worst happened. I didn't go to Pam's funeral. I'd said goodbye to her attached to that machine. Seeing her not alive, was out of the question. Pamela Howell (S.I.P.)

By New Year's Rita, was already 6 months' pregnant with our daughter. My last album Trial and Error was a huge success in my eyes. Friends, family and strangers were all fans and I'd made tens of thousands off the disc over the course of one year.

I wanted to make a new album but, the new standard was, "Mixtape, then album"

"S.O.A.L. Survivor Vol. 3 The Truth is in The Proof".

I'd done all my pre-production, so I'd already heard the mixtape. It was my best one yet, I was in a zone. It ended up taking 2 weeks.

When I got home, I was greeted by a sexy 7-month pregnant Rita in a white negligee with hearts all over it, a matching thong, red heels with clips running up the side of her lace see through robe. It was Valentine's Day and her plan worked like a charm. I squeezed whatever I could reach, and kissed her like I missed her, because I did. She took off laughing, trying to get away telling me, "Nope, no, wait, that's later". She sat me down in the living room and brought me a well-dressed plate, lit a candle, sat with me and asked what I thought about the food, because I'd only taken a few bites. I couldn't take my eyes off her. She had makeup on. She never wore makeup. She'd done her own hair, one side corn rowed and the other side Shirley Templed. She'd done it like that once before and I complimented her, telling her how dope I thought it was.

I was locked on her. She smiled, picked up my fork and put a scoop in my mouth. I kept my eyes locked on her. She smiled, got up grabbed my hand and said, "Okay, come on", and walked me into the bedroom. I followed that big wiggly butt as she paused midway, pointed at the food and said, "You better eat that". I quicknodded yes, guidng her into the room.

The first thing I saw when I walked into the hospital delivery room was my daughter's face over the doctor's shoulder, with his back facing the door. Jakaya was already about 3 minutes old, and I'd missed it.

Rita called me and I'd gotten there as fast as I could but, my daughter was already there among the room's occupants.

I smiled looking up at her as her tiny head leaned over the doctor's shoulder. She looked me up and down, then turned her head while rolling her eyes. I thought; did I see what I just saw? I was taken aback. What I got from her look was, "Oh, him? This is the father?".

I walked in checking on Rita, then my daughter and they both gave me attitude. I apologized, explained myself, and they forgave me. I held Jakaya Saddler born April 12th, 2006, fed her, stared at the female version of my son's face with a full head of hair, perfectly puffed in a curly afro and was ready to immediately begin serving my little princess.

We got our daughter home, layed her down on her stomach, stood side by side and stared at her.

She must've sensed it because just then, she got up on her hands and started swiveling her neck, slowly left to right, scanning the room. With a confused look, I asked Rita, "Didn't the doctor say she'd be doing that in a couple of weeks?". With a shocked look, she laughed and said "Yeah". And that's how it stayed; my daughter wanted to be acknowledged. She walked early, talked early, was always the smallest thing in the room, but you couldn't miss her. When she would drool, I'd lay on my back, hold her up in the air and let the spit drip into my mouth. It tasted exactly like Poland spring water. I parted with her shortly for the first time and it was hard but, I had to go to Satannie's to go pick up Jada and Lil Joe.

I had a family to support, so I got right back to work.

As a father of 3, plus a woman; the mother of my children depending on me, there's really no room for, "I don't have it". It's either, you've already got it, or you're just on your way to go get it. That's if you want a fully functioning family structure.

I kept up working at the Driving school, winging it with my fathering skills and Rita did what she could as a mom of 3 babies.

There's a reason I believe, through all these instances of curves and circumstances that Rita and I were forced into each other's lives.

Maybe one day that reason will reveal itself.

Maybe it already has, and I missed it.

Maybe it is, and I'm just not getting it.

Rita'd come from a turbulent and dysfunctional background and even though I was raised by my mother, and my father's an international celebrity, I was as, if not more, screwed up than she was.

I couldn't be what she needed me to be, just like she couldn't be what I needed her to be. We did our best, but it wasn't enough because, we just didn't know how.

Rita and I slowly fell apart after the 2nd baby and I'd stopped making music but, so far, I'd done either an album or a mixtape every year since 2002, plus the album I did with my dad a couple years earlier. It was 2007 and I didn't want the year to go by without a JayFlo offering so, I paid for studio time, put together a sort of greatest hits c.d. using the songs I got the most comments about, added 3 new tracks and called it JayFlo.com to steer people toward my new website.

Rita and I broke up but, I knew I still had to be there for my kids, no matter what. And I am.

February /2008.

Rita and I stayed separated but, we did everything for the kids and took care of them like we were still a family unit. I'd even stay over sometimes.

Around this same time, my father reaches out to me wanting me to do a song on his upcoming album called, "The Bridge". I hadn't seen or spoken to my father in years. I was skeptical but, I guess the pain of our last interaction had worn off and I said cool.

I'd never stopped rapping. It was who I was, and this was an opportunity. I didn't take it that serious because it concerned my dad but, I was going to do it, give it my all and whatever happens, happens.

I drove down to my dad's house in Central Islip Long Island.

To look at his wall in his office, you'd think he was this involved, family-oriented person. He had pictures of me, my siblings and all his grandchildren. The pictures to me looked like perfectly shot photo ops. No warm kick around, average day pics and I owned no pictures of him. I guess he felt if he couldn't see us in the flesh, at least he still gets to see us.

I went to the basement studio, sat down and he played me some beats. I couldn't front, he'd gotten a lot better at beat making.

Track after track for me was thought provoking, so I knew he had something. I picked this soft slow beat because, I'd written this song called; "Woman", (which he refuses to give me a copy of, or anything else I've done with him; shows etc.) and it's like this was the beat I'd been hearing in my head to it. I laid it down and everybody that was there loved it.

It was time for me to go but, before I left, he played a beat he had prepared for some other dude, and as soon as I heard it, I knew I had to be a part of it. I said, "What you doin wit that one?"/ "Nothin yet". It was the opposite of "Woman". This beat was hard. I started writing right there. I wanted to have 2 different types of songs on the album if I could, and I told him so. He said, "Well, lets see what you've got".

I went in the booth and ran right through it. The hook was already on it and ended up being called; "I Got Something to Say". We walked upstairs to the main part of the house, talked for a little and I was ready to go. I told my dad; "You know, Mann, Ricky and Michelle might feel left out if you don't include them somehow". He had no response except light laughter. He then said to me that he was glad I was still doing my thing and I should realize, that if I was serious about getting into the music business, I was going to have to make a "Sacrifice".

He then said, "The sacrifice I had to make, was being around yall".

I nodded my head in agreement, but when his statement settled into my brain I was confused, and my whole life flashed before my eyes.

If I didn't know before, I knew right there and then, I'd never put anything, or anybody before my son and my daughter.

Months later, one day I went to the supermarket and there it was.

My picture in the XXL Magazine, and an article all about, Me.

Georgette Cline, a writer for XXL called me and conducted a phone interview. My father's album was about to drop. He'd previously told me about the phone interview, wanted to give me some tips on how to conduct myself and gave me a few suggestions.

By now it was 2009 and one of his suggestions was for me to lie about my age, which I don't blame him for saying because at the time I was 33, and if you go by the industry standard, I'd already aged out by at least 10 years.

I didn't want to tell any lies though. The business I felt, came with enough stress. Remembering and trying to keep lies in order, was an unnecessarily added burden. I'd rather just be myself, accepted or rejected. I was so proud of what I'd accomplished.

To get to this point of having my musical contribution spoken of in an international magazine gave me a great sense of validation.

I had a good amount of money saved up and with the publicity of my album in the XXL, I'd gotten the motivation to finally finish recording my album; "Son of a Legend" from my S.OA.L. Survivor mixtape trilogy. I had an ill idea for an album cover too.

I went to get 2 T-shirts made, one for me and one for my son. Black Tee's with lettering on the front that said, "The Son", on Lil Joe's shirt and, "The Legend", on mine. Everyone looking at the cover would've thought I was talking about my dad by calling it Son of a Legend but, when you opened the cover, you'd see Lil Joe sitting on the throne with his shirt that said, "The Son", and me standing beside him, wearing my shirt that said, "The Legend".

I was hyped. Only thing left to do, was make the cover.

-Chapter Twelve-

<u>New Respect</u>

My music was the only thing I had to keep me from losing my mind and I was ready to finally finish and put it out. It was amazing.

Track for track. I was totally shocked by the ideas, thoughts and concepts that made my album come together, I always am. When it's good. I always feel blessed that I was given this great gift of mixing and measuring words to create an audio entrée, with my own secret recipe. It's always kept me safe, and caused me to want to understand the world, the people, animals and even the insects in it.

Since I've been aware of purpose, I've felt like HipHop was mine. This album was the best I'd done so far, and I was ready. Hopefully this time, if I worked hard, and got lucky, I'd get the deal I'd spent the last 20 years chasing.

I had to make sure everything was straight with the kids before I started making my moves. I couldn't do to them, what my father did to me.

I warned against Rita spending time with her old friends, and it quickly caught up with her. She got jammed up, arrested, and I ended up having to take over until they were to let her go. Jakaya was 3 LilJoe was 6 and Jada who at the time was 12 ended up with her dad's side of the family, since legally, I had no rights to her.

It was tough doing everything by myself but, it forced me to gain a new respect for my mother, and any woman that was a single person raising a child alone. I did with the situation, the same as I've done with many situations throughout my life. I put it in a song, wrote it and called it; "New Respect". I was evolving.

I never took credit for doing my job as a father but, the fact remains. A high percentage of children do not have their fathers playing active roles in their lives. I was one of those kids. I chose to be a part of the solution.

I told a lady at my new job at the hospital I wanted to cook Thanksgiving for my kids so, she wrote down exactly how I had to prepare everything on a sheet of paper.

I cooked everything; Baked macaroni and cheese, Lasagne, Collard greens, Stuffing, a cake, a couple of pies, corn bread and last, but not least, Turkey, that we couldn't eat because I burned it but, I went and bought a whole chicken that was already cooked, and we used that.

The kids were growing mentally, physically and had a huge amount of energy being so young. They were live.

It was tough but, honestly, I felt so blessed. The kids made it easy to feel that way. They knew exactly what was going on and never felt down about it so, that kept me in good spirits. I had money, and we always ate good. We went to the movies, the park and always had activities.

No matter how much I tried to explain to them "Everything is going to be alright" they'd say things like; "Daddy, we gotta do what we gotta do".

I stopped by moms in the Bronx a couple weeks after Thanksgiving and my mom told Satannie that I'd stopped by. Satannie called to set up a meeting with me and I wanted to see my niece and nephew so, I was all for it.

The weekend was here so we met at a salon on Simpson St. in The Bronx by the 2 train where my neice was getting her hair done. I was happy to see Satannie, and the kids were all happy to see each other. We sat, we talked and waited 'til Neicee's hair was done.

About 20 minutes into our reunion, a white BMW pulls up and my father hops out. He says, "What's up son?", hugged me and had that same smell he's had since I was a little kid, I don't know if it was still Joop but, to me, it always smelled like money.

I had mixed feelings about him and didn't appreciate Satannie calling him there without telling me. I unenthusiastically said, "Hey, what's up?". He was in good spirits and the kids were happy to see him so, I wasn't going to spoil it. He asked how I was doing, and I told him, exactly. As usual, he couldn't stay because he was busy, but would set aside some time for us to sit and talk the following day. I said cool.

I don't know why but, I still had hope that maybe my father would one day come to my rescue. I needed it now more than ever. We said our goodbyes and they pulled off.

The kids wanted to stop at the store before we went back upstairs. At that age they were so easy to please. That's all they ever wanted. A few snacks and they were good.

The next day, I met with my father at Dunkin Donuts on Zerega Ave. in the Bronx.

What I didn't know at the time was, it would be 5 years from that day, before I got to see or speak to my father again.

It had been 2 years since I'd last seen him that day and, before that, it was 4. As I looked at him talking, it made me think about something.

If I added up all the days in my entire life and how many times I'd sat face to face with him, like we were in that moment, it wouldn't have added up to more than 3 months, total. I knew barely anything about him. I didn't know he wasn't born in the Bronx or that he was a Jehovah's witness.

Still, no matter how old I got, I craved that father/son relationship as much as I did when I was a little boy. I don't know why but, that feeling just wouldn't go away. To laugh with him, to sit and do nothing, to talk and joke. I've been through so much and have overcome so many obstacles but, that flat piece of cement lays weighing down on my chest. Like music, it's a part of me, another one of my arteries.

I let my guard down as usual, began talking about my music and how I had a new sound... and a new name. I told him my name wasn't JayFlo anymore.

He asked, "So what is it?". I said, "JoeJoe Dawson". He crunched his face up like something stunk and said "Ooo Joe". He loved it. He said, "Okay Joseph Saddler..." calling me by my government name "...why JoeJoe Dawson?"/ "Well, I already got your name so, I wanted to use my mothers name."/ "Wow Joe, dope. Let me hear the music". He suggested years ago I dumb it down and since that's how a lot of the music on the radio was, I gave in.

I decided it wasn't about being the best rapper anymore. I had 2 children to support, and really needed to get on. I'd spent my whole life making music and, I didn't know how, nor did I want to do anything else.

My father heard the change in my sound and liked the music as much as anyone I'd previously played it for but, gave me every reason why it would never work.

He brought up how it costs money for promotions, production, I needed connections for features, me having the kids by myself would get in the way, yadda yadda yadda. He never once came up with a way we could make it work.

I myself know, there's always a way to make something work, if you work hard enough at it.

He's never helped anyone but himself and it finally set in... I wasn't gonna be an exception.

I then thought to myself; "Why did he have us meet at a Dunkin Donuts, instead of his house?".

He was the same. My father was not interested in me.

To me, I felt like he was only there to see what I was up to and still saw me as a threat. He was just checking out, what he feels is his competition

I kept it cool, had a few more minutes of empty chatter, grabbed my c.d. and told him I needed to head out. He was upbeat, said bye to the kids, pulled out $300 and handed it to me. I reluctantly accepted because I had the kids and knew I could use it.

I felt humiliated, ashamed and embarrassed that I'd been in such a vulnerable position. I thanked him, gave him a hug, a pound, got the kids and headed to my car.

After I was better situated with the kids, I got my old job back at Grand Prix. Found a place about an hour outside of NYC in Poughkeepsie NY and paid $2700 for first, last month's rent. The Bronx has always been rough. I adapted. I did not want my kids to.

It was a blessing because, at least I didn't have to buy any new furniture. We were already fully furnished from our previous place.

The kids liked the house but didn't like being outside of New York City because, they always got to see their cousins. My aunt Barbara always did things with them, and they loved their schools.

By this time, my daughter was 6 and Joe was 9. I'd had them for almost 3 years by myself before their mom got them back.

I kept working at Grand Prix.

I'd finally, after years of struggling gotten to a point in my life, where I felt proud of myself. I was ready to move forward toward joy, and away from my pain. I'd come a long way.

A year later I decided once again, I wanted to cook Thanksgiving for the kids so, I went food shopping, got them a new Xbox system, a few games and enjoyed the holiday. This time, I didn't attempt a Turkey, I cooked a huge spread and baked a whole chicken. We had great times in that house but, things were about to change, drastically.

-Chapter Thirteen-
A Child is Born...

It took me years to build the home I'd built for my children and I. In a matter of hours, it was reduced to rubble.

February 24th, 2016, I came home, my door was kicked in, and everything was gone. Flat screens, laptops, over 30 pairs of sneakers some I hadn't worn yet, leather jackets, clothes I hadn't worn yet, $1600 in cash, everything, gone. Promotional items like my posters and T-shirts with my logo on it, gone. My laptop and my tablets contained all the music I'd ever done in my life, because I transferred them over from my c.d.'s, gone. Pictures of my son and my daughter from the day they were born, up until that point. I'd transferred those over from my cellphone, gone.

This was the last straw.

I'd reached my breaking point.

I took a second, looked, and realized, pain had been with me my whole life, following me around.

I started writing my book as a kid when I thought I was going to be a big rap star and kept notebooks; one of the few things left scattered in the rubble after the burglary.

I grabbed the loose pages, began collecting my scribed experiences. Organized my old life and created a foundation for my new one.

God has a plan. I believe that. My place looked like a hurricane hit it, and I'd always kept my place very neat. I sat in the aftermath, knowing there was a reason for all of this. What it was. I had no clue, yet. I knew one thing for sure, this person not only took my things, but they also stole my security, my confidence and peace of mind. I stood up and looked around at my own personal 9/11 and walked out the door, determined to get my life back in order. I had 2 children depending on me, no time to wallow.

I gave my father one last chance at us having a relationship, the week DMX (S.I.P.) passed away. I hadn't seen or spoken to my dad in 6 years.

So many hiphop artist kept dying back-to-back. I didn't want to wake up one morning and hear that about my father, so I decided to reach out to him because I knew from experience that he'd never reach out to me. I kept the contact very lighthearted, called him, and as soon as he picked up the phone I gleefully spouted "what's up Pops" as if we'd been speaking everyday, when in reality, it had been years. He said, "Hey son I was just thinking about you last week". In my mind the only thought was (but you didn't call).

I kept that thought to myself and went into that time we'd pranked him in New Jersey with the fake poop to see if he remembered. After I told the story he asked how I was doing but like I said I wanted to keep it light and said to him cheerfully; "Everythings good, im not gon take up your time, just wanted to share that with you but, I gotta go, got some errands to run". He said "Cool son, just make sure you keep in touch. When you get a minute, text me the kids phone numbers so I can call them". I said "cool". With no intentions on honoring his request. I wanted to take babysteps.

My father wanted things his way and immediately started texting me after the lighthearted phone call…

…our conversation went like this.

(Flash): "Send me the kid's numbers"

(Me): "I'm super protective of my kids Pops. I don't want them getting too overly excited about you, know what I mean? Let me talk to them first and next time I have them I'll allow you all to speak. We'll take it from there"

(Flash): "No prob"

I kinda felt from his response, that it was a "prob".

(Me): "Cool. I won't act like it didn't bother me when you sent money to Rita without asking or notifying me and making visit plans. I just want things like that when it comes to the kids to go through me. I'm your family not Rita. And the kids don't run nothing. I want you to see them. I would just appreciate proper protocol."

(Flash): "Hey son I'm not one to be in you and Rita's business that's not me, but if it affects your kids I'm there everytime. We're both grown son. All I can say is disappearing is not helpful. We don't have no beef. Im clear they are your kids but you all have MY blood and if I get the call, im there everytime real talk son. Protocols are for friends, homeboys or peoples. Which I am not."

(Me): "I respect your view. I won't try to change it. I accept it. Hopefully, you respect mine. Its no disrespect. Its just how I handle things. In my view, its wrong to deal with Rita opposed to me. Rita and I are fine. We focus strictly on our children."

(Flash): "Like I said son; you and Rita are none of my biz. If the kids need grandpa im there everytime. If we stay in touch from time to time that takes Rita out of OUR picture. Fyi those kids are my fam just as much as you are, that's the protocol. Stay in touch and I promise to do the same. Miss ya man."

(Me): "I don't think you understand. Youre a boss where you are. You call all the shots in your life. I'm the boss over here. Respectfully. No man dictates my situation in any way. I didn't reach out to fight with you. If you can't just be a humble guest, nod and agree with what I've built, you won't be welcome. It's up to you. I am the boss Pops. Do not go over or around me or we will have a problem. Which I don't want.".

At this point he stops texting and immediately calls me. I know what he wanted. It felt familiar. Insults, shots, degradation... yeah, I remember. He didn't like having what he feels is his "authority" being challenged by me. His life has been filled with kiss-asses. He hates that I was never one of em'. He's so stuck on his "Father" title that he doesn't realize it means nothing to me now that im a father and know what a real father does. Until he respects me as his peer, 2 grown men, we'll never get along.

So, I declined the call from my recliner in my living room and texted...

(Me): Drivin

(Flash): "Okay cool, call when possible"

(Me): "Okay but keep in mind I just called to tell you a funny story. I stay clear of anybody with the last name Dawson or Saddler because they always hurt me, and each other. Always have. I don't need that. I have PEACE of mind now and have for a very long time. I hope whatever you're goona say doesn't disturb that. If it is you can keep it to yourself. Just let me be. I reached out to share a funny story. It's all I wanted. Nothing more. So, choose your words carefully."

(Flash): "It's fine Joe if staying clear is the answer I'm gonna have to accept that. Thanks for calling. I'm a Saddler, always will be."

(Me): "So that's all you got from what I just said? I'm confused. Did you just skim through Deepak Chopra?"

He'd told me he read, Deepak Chopra. Which gave me an interest in Deepak Chopra.

(Me): "Anyway, this went nowhere and the energy's no good. At least we had a good laugh. Bye."

(Flash): "I'm a guest?! I'M THE BOSS?! Choose My Word CAREFULLY?! So disrespectful. The same problems you're having with your son youre having with me. Protocol. Father respect. Son respect. Even if we disagree. Im never gonna be a guest, or choose words wisely, this aint Germany and you aint Hitler. In other words, you can say whatever and its fine? Yes, this went nowhere. You started with a JOKE and ended up being a JOKE. Be well son."

(Me): "You can't compare mine and your situation. My son and I have a real relationship and a genuine history. You and I do not. You want control. I have it. I have no problem with you. I'm just being real. Why attack me? This is your chance. You're blowing it. I don't want to argue. It's too typical. Have you not found peace yet? I really am not trying to hurt you. I just need you to respect my boundaries instead of trying to just do things your own way. My children are my children. I make the rules. You do not. Why attack me and try to hurt me? You see?"

(Flash): "OK, I'm good son".

After that he blocked me: April 25, 2021, 12 days after my birthday.

It's the last time I've heard from him.

2 months later in June, he threw a Birthday party for my cousin that is not, his nephew. My mother's nephew who I was always the closest with growing up. I wasn't invited. I thought long and hard and honestly, I can't remember my father ever saying Happy Birthday to me. I know for sure I've never seen him on my birthday. My fathers been my enemy this whole time and I was so blinded by me wanting a father-son relationship that I never stopped to consider, he'd been planning my downfall from the very beginning.

He even recruited my flesh and blood sister Satannie, some of my friends and a few of my starstruck family members to assist in doing his bidding. I would proudly tell all my plans to them. I was wide opened to my family. Fully trusting. The whole time they were feeding him info keeping him a step ahead of me and I was totally oblivious.

What he doesn't realize is him holding me back is why he himself has yet to succeed. You can't hold somebody back without staying back with them. To the naked eye, he's successful. In honesty, he's his own biggest fan living off the fumes of something he may or may not have done almost half a century ago. He gets honorable mentions from every artist and industry bigwig you could name but none of them give him work, opportunity or any real looks. He comes around my relatives to shine bright amongst poor people. And let's not forget the most important factor... With this next statement I don't speak for any of my siblings. I'll speak for me.

I will NEVER... EVER... respect a man that doesn't take care of his children.

Dame Dash worded it perfectly for me when he said, "Hustle for your last name, not your first name", I'll admit I didn't get that jewel when he first dropped it but once I did, I just thought... Wow, that's how I'm naturally wired.

I may be a little bit delirious right now but, I'm happy. When I say im happy it's because when I'm sad I cry, real tears. I sometimes even cry happy tears. When I'm feeling down, I go through it in stride. When I'm feeling lonely, I accept. When I'm angry, I endure.

I remind myself... In this life, I got to be in love. In love with a woman for 10 years. Made 2 children, raised a third and was blessed with this beautiful gift to create. I got to spend time with my father, while I have friends who've never met their dad or even know who their dad is. I've had friends, siblings, extended family and have even come across the inconsequential stranger who's made a rainy day feel sunny. I have memories, great ones that exclude extravagance and blossoms in the basic. I'm not exempt from pain or depression, but its not all God's offered me in this lifetime.

I'm happy to have this better understanding of how real life works.

It's all so funny to me.

How and why did all these bad things happen to me, I'm okay with it, and have no bad feelings toward anybody?

I don't understand why, so, maybe after reading this, someone can figure it out and explain it to me.

My life made me the way I am and, other peoples lives made them. I'm a man so, I feel, if a man is not taught by an experienced, elder male, Father, Uncle, Grandfather etc. he will lack the key tools it takes to become a man.

A boy can emulate his father but, if a boy through his transition can live up to his mother's expectation, and his father is consistent throughout the process, without him even knowing it, he will have become a proper man.

I've learned a lot throughout the course of my life, about myself and life in general. No one man or woman taught me. I've learned every lesson the hard way. By going through it.

I've come across some good luck every now and then and count all my blessings. I'm still here while so many are gone. Through everything I've been through and the pain I suffered I gained the opportunity to see my strength and I made it through. The greatest pain has now gotten me to appreciate the simplest pleasures. Something as simple as a moment of peace, where nothing is wrong and nothing bad is happening brings me joy and I take full advantage, always. I smile, crack jokes, laugh and appreciate.

I've also learned to not internalize or let what I feel and think, take presidence over what's truly real. Hate is done on a whim and takes no real effort. To be positive, it takes work. To love, it takes time with no instant gratification and a long challenging road, full of unavoidable pain, suffering and sacrifice. The glory of love shines brightest and truly flourishes at the end of the journey.

I didn't know why I wrote this book when I first began. Reflecting on my life, its tests, trials and challenges. I've come out on the other end knowing that the most important part of my existence is being myself. No matter what anyone says or thinks about me. Being the imperfect me that I am. I've been wrong, I've been right. After reading this book, you may hate me, you may love me, hell, you may even understand me but, in this book, you got all of me, the true me I was afraid to be.

The greatest HipHop verse I've ever heard was said by Melle Mel. It starts with "A Child is born...". Its timeless. Still relevant almost a half a century after its conception. I was born with no state of mind, blind to the ways of mankind, became a man and... I'm here.

I know now why I wrote this book... To set myself free.

From this day forward, I'm free.

Free to be...

Me.

The ~~end~~ beginning.

The Dozen Do's

1. The hardest part of any task is getting started. If you want to finish, start.

2. Learn yourself, know yourself, love yourself.

3. Life is only short if you waste the days you're given.

4. When dealing with people, don't ignore the signs. Good or bad.

5. When planning, plan, ahead of your plan.

6. Loss happens. Accept it. Time spent on losses could've been spent on gaining.

7. Success doesn't happen over night. The "Image" of success does. Make the necessary sacrifices. Do the work. Enjoy the ride.

8. Silence can be a dangerous sound. Speak up.

9. True power lies in the people and the lives you touch.

10. Don't always look outside for the answer. Look inside yourself.

11. Be loyal, not blind.

12. The road to success is a lonely one. (Refer to #2)

Thank you all for your support.

It is greatly appreciated.

(All music available on all streaming sites)

StraightHood

Keep Dreaming

The L.O.V.E.

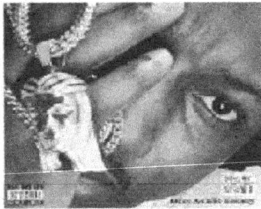
Here As the Enemy

Once Upon a Time in... 2005

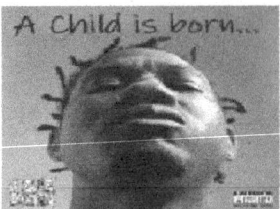
A Child is born...

Cantletchustopit!

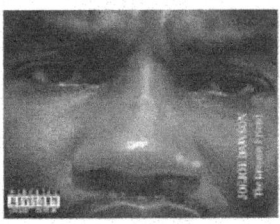
The Acapellas

God Music Family

(More music on **datpiff.com**)

All music

Written & Produced by

JoeJoe Dawson

For

Now You C entertainment

Peeeace!!!